Foreword

*I*n the OECD Directorate for Education, we are very aware of the key role played by knowledge management in a world of information overload and knowledge-based economies. Traditionally, as OECD analyses have shown, education has not been exemplar in its own knowledge management, despite "knowledge" being education's core business.

We have applied this observation to our own work. We have become aware that despite – or because of – our continued energetic output of publications there was need to create greater transparency about the key messages from our output as a whole. We have identified the need to present these in an accessible way so that they can be used by different audiences – our own national contacts, other sections of governments, experts, media, and the wider public – who do not have the time to tackle the full corpus of international analysis coming out of our Directorate. Few users read OECD reports cover to cover: this report represents a resource in modular format to help readers to dip in and out and take from it those findings of most interest to them.

We have limited the scope of this resource so that it includes only published results and policy orientations, and those applicable to most OECD countries (rather, for example, than single country reviews). The coverage includes some analyses that have depended on other Directorates in OECD with a direct interest in education in cases where these have been published, at least jointly, by the Directorate for Education.

This is a "first" of its kind for the OECD Directorate for Education. We intend to update it at regular intervals but not to publish every year – how frequently it will be published and in what format will depend in part on the reception this initial edition receives. Within the Directorate for Education, this synthesis has been undertaken by the Centre for Educational Research and Innovation (CERI) and future updating is included in the CERI programme. It was prepared by David Istance, with Delphine Grandrieux who was responsible for copy-editing and Eric Charbonnier and Corinne Heckmann who provided the statistical graphics.

Barbara Ischinger, Director
Directorate for Education

Education Today

THE OECD PERSPECTIVE

OECD

ORGANISATION FOR ECONOMIC CO-OPERATION AND DEVELOPMENT

The OECD is a unique forum where the governments of 30 democracies work together to address the economic, social and environmental challenges of globalisation. The OECD is also at the forefront of efforts to understand and to help governments respond to new developments and concerns, such as corporate governance, the information economy and the challenges of an ageing population. The Organisation provides a setting where governments can compare policy experiences, seek answers to common problems, identify good practice and work to co-ordinate domestic and international policies.

The OECD member countries are: Australia, Austria, Belgium, Canada, the Czech Republic, Denmark, Finland, France, Germany, Greece, Hungary, Iceland, Ireland, Italy, Japan, Korea, Luxembourg, Mexico, the Netherlands, New Zealand, Norway, Poland, Portugal, the Slovak Republic, Spain, Sweden, Switzerland, Turkey, the United Kingdom and the United States. The Commission of the European Communities takes part in the work of the OECD.

OECD Publishing disseminates widely the results of the Organisation's statistics gathering and research on economic, social and environmental issues, as well as the conventions, guidelines and standards agreed by its members.

This work is published on the responsibility of the Secretary-General of the OECD. The opinions expressed and arguments employed herein do not necessarily reflect the official views of the Organisation or of the governments of its member countries.

Also available in French under the title:
L'éducation aujourd'hui
LA PERSPECTIVE DE L'OCDE

Table of Contents

Introduction   7

Chapter 1. **Early Childhood Education and Care**   9
    1.1. Key findings and conclusions   10
    1.2. Orientations for policy   14

Chapter 2. **Schooling – Investments, Organisation, and Learners**   17
    2.1. Key findings and conclusions   18
    2.2. Orientations for policy   25

Chapter 3. **Transitions beyond Initial Education**   31
    3.1. Key findings and conclusions   32
    3.2. Orientations for policy   36

Chapter 4. **Higher Education**   39
    4.1. Key findings and conclusions   40
    4.2. Orientations for policy   45

Chapter 5. **Adult Education and Training – Participation and Provision**   51
    5.1. Key findings and conclusions   52
    5.2. Orientations for policy   55

Chapter 6. **Lifelong Learning**   59
    6.1. Key findings and conclusions   60
    6.2. Orientations for policy   62

Chapter 7. **Outcomes, Benefits and Returns**   65
    7.1. Key findings and conclusions   66
    7.2. Orientations for policy   74

Chapter 8. **Equity and Equality of Opportunity**   77
    8.1. Key findings and conclusions   78
    8.2. Orientations for policy   82

Chapter 9. **Innovation and Knowledge Management**   87
    9.1. Key findings and conclusions   88
    9.2. Orientations for policy   89

Bibliography   93

List of tables
    1.1. Main forms of funding for early childhood education
          and care services   12

List of figures

1.1. Most children come into education well before the age
of 5 years (2006) 10

2.1. Spending per school student going up. 20

2.2. Total number of intended instruction hours
in public institutions between the ages of 7 and 14 (2006) 21

3.1. Completion of upper secondary education
is now the norm across OECD countries 34

3.2. Expected years in education and not in education
for 15-to-29-year-olds (2006) 35

4.1. Population that has attained at least tertiary education (2006) 40

4.2. Distribution of foreign students in tertiary education,
by country of destination (2006) 43

5.1. Adults enrolled in education (2006) 53

6.1. Expected time in education for 5-year-olds based on current
enrolment patterns (2004) 61

7.1. Percentages in each PISA proficiency level in science (2006) 67

7.2. Percentages in each PISA proficiency level
in mathematics (2006) 68

7.3. Percentages in each PISA proficiency level in reading (2006) 68

7.4. Earnings from employment by level of educational
attainment for 25-to-64-years-olds by gender,
2006 or latest available year 71

8.1. Women have overtaken men in upper secondary and higher
education attainments, as shown by attainments
of different age groups in the adult population in 2006 80

8.2. Mathematics performance by migration status in 2003 80

This book has...

StatLinks

A service that delivers Excel® files from the printed page!

Look for the *StatLinks* at the bottom right-hand corner of the tables or graphs in this book.
To download the matching Excel® spreadsheet, just type the link into your Internet browser,
starting with the *http://dx.doi.org* prefix.
If you're reading the PDF e-book edition, and your PC is connected to the Internet, simply
click on the link. You'll find *StatLinks* appearing in more OECD books.

EDUCATION TODAY: THE OECD PERSPECTIVE – ISBN 978-92-64-05989-4 – © OECD 2009

Introduction

This summary report is based on results from OECD work produced primarily since 2002 when the Directorate for Education was created, and especially in the past 3-4 years. The background to its preparation is explained in the Foreword by Director Barbara Ischinger. The approach chosen focuses on results and policy orientations which are published and hence in the public domain. Only generalised findings about developments, policy, or practice relevant across most OECD countries have been included. So, not covered are: studies or reviews of single countries; publications which provide exchange of information on promising practice without broader analytic conclusions; work plans and programme intentions; clarifying statements of problems/challenges/issues.

It is divided into nine sections, devised as a structure to reflect well the different areas of educational work and to bring out policy conclusions and messages. The choice of a larger number of short sections is deliberate in order to allow the key messages to emerge more clearly than they would in a smaller number of extensive "chapters". We have also included some illustrative charts as visuals to complement the text.

It is produced entirely in modular format rather than as a continuous narrative. Each of the sections is divided into, respectively: *Key findings and conclusions* and *Orientations for policy*. Each modular text is introduced by the key message it contains or, where the module is in the form of a list of messages, these are highlighted instead. Each one also includes the title and chapter reference to the OECD report from which it comes, and these titles are brought together in an extensive but not exhaustive bibliography at the end.

In order to stay within manageable limits, this resource is highly selective of all the possible findings and policy orientations regarding education at OECD. As the included texts are removed from the fuller analyses from which they are taken, there is a natural risk of over-simplification with short conclusions taken out of their wider analytical context. For both of these reasons, therefore, it is strongly advised that users looking for more than the headline messages should refer back to the original OECD source for the fuller picture.

ISBN 978-92-64-05989-4
Education Today
The OECD Perspective
© OECD 2009

Chapter 1

Early Childhood Education and Care

Early childhood provision – pre-primary and childcare – has been a growing priority in many countries. Such priority is manifest by demanding parents, and it is also a phase of education and services increasingly recognised as important in its contribution to a wide range of social, economic and educational goals. At the same time, it is a sector with a complex diversity of players and partners and one with a significant lack of investment in many countries. A major OECD review in the field of early childhood published by OECD in 2006 – Starting Strong II: Early Childhood Education and Care – was a follow-up to an earlier international review published in 2001. Its policy orientations are broadly focused on overcoming the under-developed status of the sector that remains typical of many countries.

1.1. Key findings and conclusions

In the majority of countries – but not all – education now begins for most well before 5 years old: Already over two-thirds of the age group of young children aged 3 and 4 years (69.4%) are enrolled in education across OECD countries as a whole. Enrolment rates for early childhood education at this age range from over 90% in Belgium, Denmark, France, Germany, Iceland, Italy, New Zealand, Spain, and the United Kingdom, at one end of the spectrum, to less than a quarter in Ireland, Korea and Turkey.

📖 *Education at a Glance: OECD Indicators – 2008 Edition*, Chapter C.

Figure 1.1. **Most children come into education well before the age of 5 years (2006)**

Children 4 years and younger in education as a percentage of 3- and 4-year-olds

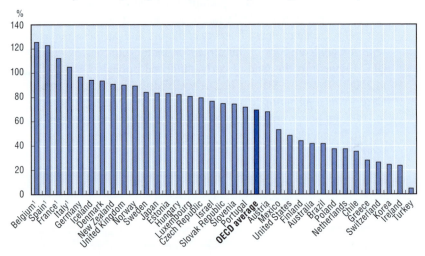

1. In some countries, there is a significant number of children younger than 3 years old in education; this accounts for percentages in excess of 100%.

Source: OECD (2008), *Education at a Glance: OECD Indicators – 2008 Edition*, OECD Publishing, Paris.

StatLink ⟐🖾 http://dx.doi.org/10.1787/402156412821

Demand for early childhood provision for those aged under 3 years far outstrips supply in all but the Nordic region: The highest levels of enrolment of infants under 3 years of age in early childhood education and care in publicly subsidised provision are in Denmark and Sweden. Apart from these two

EDUCATION TODAY: THE OECD PERSPECTIVE – ISBN 978-92-64-05989-4 – © OECD 2009

countries and Finland, the evidence of OECD reviews shows that the demand for services for young children is significantly higher than the places available, even in countries with provision for long parental leave. In countries where public funding for such provision is limited, most working parents must either seek solutions in the private market, where ability to pay significantly influences accessibility to quality services, or else rely on informal arrangements with family, friends and neighbours. The publicly-subsidised services for these young children take several forms: family day care, centre-based crèche services and integrated services.

📖 *Starting Strong II: Early Childhood Education and Care*, 2006, Chapter 4.

Publicly-funded pre-primary provision tends to be more strongly developed in the European than in the non-European countries of the OECD: In Europe, the concept of universal access of 3- to 6-year-olds is generally accepted. Most countries in this region provide all children with at least two years of free, publicly-funded provision before they begin primary provision. With the exception of Ireland and the Netherlands, such access is generally a statutory right from the age of 3 years and in some even before that. Early education programmes in Europe are often free and attached to schools. In OECD countries outside Europe, free early education tends to be only available from age 5, though many children are enrolled from age 4 in Australia, Korea and some US states.

📖 *Starting Strong II: Early Childhood Education and Care*, 2006, Chapter 4.

Two broad emphases in early education characterise different countries – preparing for school and social pedagogy: OECD countries approach the partnership between early childhood services and the primary school in different ways – all trying to improve the co-ordination between the sectors but starting from different premises. Broadly, there are two different approaches across countries. France and the English-speaking countries tend to see the question of partnership from the point of view of the school: early education should serve the objectives of public education and provide children with "readiness for school" skills. In contrast, countries inheriting the social pedagogy tradition (the Nordic and Central European countries) see kindergarten as a specific institution turned more to supporting families and the broad development needs of young children.

📖 *Starting Strong II: Early Childhood Education and Care*, 2006, Chapter 3.

A positive consequence of decentralisation has been the integration of early childhood education and care services at the local level, leading to a more efficient allocation of resources to children ... These new services tend to be less

Table 1.1. **Main forms of funding for early childhood education and care services (0 to 6 years) in selected countries**

	Supply funding to services	Subsidies to parents	Employer contributions
Australia	Limited to public kindergarten	Main form	Yes, tax
Belgium	Main form	Mixed in child care	Yes, employer levy
Canada	In public kindergarten and community services mainly (Provinces and Territories, to varying degrees, use also supply-side grants, operational funding, wage supplements, etc., in support of other services) Main form in Quebec	Mixed. Supply-side funding to community services is usual.	No
Denmark	Main form	No	No
Finland	Main form	Mixed	No
France	Main form	Mixed for early childhood education and care outside the *école maternelle*	Yes, employer levy
Germany	Main form	Mixed in child care	No
Hungary	Main form in child care and kindergarten	No	No
Ireland	Limited to social nurseries and public early education	Limited, mostly parental contributions	No
Italy	Main form	No	Yes, employer levy
Korea	Limited to public kindergarten, and to public targeted programme in child care centres	Main form of government support, but parental contributions are high	In some cases
Netherlands	Main form in pre-primary and targeted	Main form in child care but high parental contributions	Yes, tax to nearly 30% of costs
Norway	Main form	Mixed	Yes, tax
Portugal	Main form	Yes	Yes
Sweden	Main form	No	No
United Kingdom	Limited to public early education, social nurseries and targeted programmes	Main form for child care, but mostly parental contributions	Yes, tax
United States	Limited to public kindergarten, targeted programmes and Head Start	Main form but mostly parental contributions	Yes, tax

Source: OECD, background reports for OECD programme on early childhood education and care.

bound by traditional competency boundaries than government departments. Many local authorities in Austria, Denmark, Finland, France, Hungary, Germany, Italy, the Netherlands, Norway, Sweden, the United Kingdom and the United States have brought together children's services and education portfolios to plan more effectively and provide coherence of services for young children and their

EDUCATION TODAY: THE OECD PERSPECTIVE – ISBN 978-92-64-05989-4 – © OECD 2009

families. Some local authorities have integrated administration and policy development across age groups and sectors: in Denmark, Italy, Norway, Sweden and the United Kingdom, for example, an increasing number of local authorities have reorganised responsibility for early childhood education and care and for schools (and sometimes other children's services) under one administrative department and political committee.

... but devolution of powers and responsibilities can also widen differences of access and quality between states, regions or districts: This has occurred in Sweden but is even more evident in federal countries such as Australia, Canada, Germany and the United States, where unified national policies have been difficult to achieve. Unless strong equalising mechanisms are in place, decentralised early childhood administrations in poor urban areas can also face difficulties because of low taxation revenues. Decentralisation and well-intentioned policies in some countries (*e.g.* Canada and Hungary) have led to the creation of independent rural areas which are too small or too poor to support quality early childhood education and care services without strong state assistance. Even in situations where funding is available (such as in Australia), effective co-ordination can be inhibited by a highly dispersed population, separate state auspices for pre-school education, and a market-oriented approach to childcare.

📖 *Starting Strong II: Early Childhood Education and Care,* 2006, Chapter 2.

Disabled children and those with learning and behavioural difficulties receive less additional support at the pre-primary than at the primary level: The median percentage of the children at pre-primary level receiving additional financial resources for *disabilities* was 1.1% in 2003 – significantly lower than for children at the primary level (3.6%), though there are examples (*e.g.* the United States) of free early childhood education for disabled children. The median percentage of children in pre-primary education receiving additional resources for *learning and behavioural difficulties* is even lower at 0.3% for the countries reporting data in 2003, again with some notable exceptions (*e.g.* England [9.6%] and Chile [11.5%]). The percentage of children receiving additional resources because of *social disadvantages* was negligible in many countries with in this case the exceptions being Belgium (French Community) and Mexico, with 12.9% and 16.0% respectively.

📖 *Students with Disabilities, Learning Difficulties and Disadvantages: Policies, Statistics and Indicators – 2007 Edition,* Chapter 4.

1.2. Orientations for policy

Early childhood education and care policy needs to be systemic and integrate the different forms of early childhood provision, allow universal access, and enjoy a strong and equal partnership with the rest of the education system. The recent OECD review of this sector proposes ten policy areas for consideration:

- **Place well-being, early development and learning at the core of early childhood approaches, while respecting the child's agency and natural learning strategies:** Rather than being an adjunct to labour market policies with weak development agendas or an under-resourced "Cinderella" education service, early childhood education and care needs to have the child and its well-being and learning at the core.

- **Aspire towards early childhood education and care systems that support broad learning, participation and democracy:** The touchstones of a democratic approach are to extend the agency of the child and right of parents to be involved in the education of their children. Learning to be, learning to do, learning to learn, and learning to live together are the critical elements to be promoted in each child.

- **Provide autonomy, funding and support to early childhood services:** Within the parameters of system-wide goals and guidelines, educators and services should have the autonomy to plan and to choose curricula for the children in their care; policy should provide the means for staff to exercise such autonomy and participatory approaches.

- **Develop broad guidelines and curricular standards with the stakeholders for all early childhood education and care services:** Guiding frameworks – especially when they have been developed together by the key stakeholders – help to promote a more even quality across early childhood provision, to guide and support professional staff, and to facilitate communication between staff and families.

- **Base public funding on achieving quality pedagogical goals:** Most countries need to double their annual investment per child to ensure child-staff ratios and qualified staff be on some parity with the primary sector; the investment should be directed to achieving quality pedagogical goals rather than simply aiming to create sufficient places.

- **Improve the working conditions and professional education of early childhood education and care staff:** The OECD reviews found a number of common weaknesses that need attention: low recruitment and pay levels, particularly in child care services; lack of certification in specialist early childhood pedagogy; excessive feminisation of staff; lack of diversity of staff to reflect neighbourhood diversity.

- **Create the governance structures necessary for system accountability and quality assurance:** These include such elements as strong expert policy units, data collection and monitoring capacity, an evaluation agency, and a pedagogical advisory or inspection corps.

- **Attend to the social context of early childhood development:** Well organised services should work towards a broad but realistic vision to which the other stakeholders can subscribe, serving at the same time to support parents in child-rearing, facilitate women working, and help social inclusion for low-income and immigrant families.

- **Encourage family and community involvement in early childhood services:** The continuity of children's experience across the different early childhood education and care environments is greatly enhanced when parents and staff members share information and adopt consistent approaches to socialisation, daily routines, child development and learning; communities are important both as providers and as offering space for partnerships.

- **Reduce child poverty and exclusion through upstream fiscal, social and labour policies and increase resources within universal programmes for children with diverse learning rights:** Research indicates the effectiveness of universal programmes for children with different disabilities and disadvantages, combined with enhanced funding and investment in quality services, rather than targeted programmes which serve to segregate and stigmatise.

📖 *Starting Strong II: Early Childhood Education and Care*, 2006, Chapter 10.

ISBN 978-92-64-05989-4
Education Today
The OECD Perspective
© OECD 2009

Chapter 2

Schooling – Investments, Organisation, and Learners

The period of compulsory education – primary, lower secondary and even the upper secondary cycle in some countries – is at the core of all education systems. Over recent years, there have been significant investments in this core phase of education, recognised as being fundamental for laying the foundation on which so many other social, economic and educational outcomes may follow. Teachers (and the educational workforce in general) are widely recognised as central to the success of schooling, a position reinforced by the major 2005 OECD study Teachers Matter: Attracting, Developing and Retaining Effective Teachers. OECD work has analysed with growing precision the characteristics of learners and the nature of school practices, including leadership. Policy orientations have stressed the need simultaneously to modernise, professionalise and innovate, while also placing reforms directed at effective learning – rather than changing only structures and administrative systems – at the core of schooling.

2.1. Key findings and conclusions

Only a small minority of students do not now complete compulsory education overall, though rising to 1 in 10 in some countries: The participation rates in most OECD and partner countries tend to be high until the end of compulsory education, with more than 90% completing this phase in most. Those where more than 10% do not complete this phase of education are: Germany, Mexico, the Netherlands, New Zealand, Turkey, the United Kingdom, the United States, and partner country Chile. The age which marks the end of compulsory attendance does vary, however, and in four of these cases is relatively late at 17 or 18 years of age (Chile, Germany, the Netherlands, and the United States).

📖 *Education at a Glance: OECD Indicators – 2008 Edition*, Chapter C.

Spending on schooling – broadly defined – accounts for two-thirds (66.1%) of the total educational expenditure in OECD countries: The broad-brush measure of investment in schooling as compared with tertiary education shows that the schooling share of spending (covering pre-primary, primary, secondary and some non-tertiary, post-secondary education) accounts for two-thirds of total educational expenditure. In 2005, 70% or over is covered by the schooling portion in Ireland (74.7%), Italy (70.0%), New Zealand (70.9%), and the United Kingdom (73.9%). Tertiary education receives its highest shares in the United States (37.1%), Greece (33.5%), and Korea (33.5%) while the OECD average is less than a quarter (24.2%). (Denmark, Iceland and Japan are harder to compare as they have a sizeable proportion of spending not allocated by level – 6%, 7.7% and 7.0% respectively – while Canada, Luxembourg and Turkey do not break down expenditure by level.)

📖 *Education at a Glance: OECD Indicators – 2008 Edition*, Chapter B.

Spending per student in schooling (plus post-secondary non-tertiary) has increased everywhere in OECD countries since the mid-1990s, contrasting with a mixed picture in tertiary education: Using 100 as the index in 2000, the increase in spending per student had risen to 119 by 2005 in OECD countries and this is up from 89 in 1995. This compares with 111 for tertiary education in 2005 while the change between 1995 and 2000 averaged across all OECD countries had been negligible (99 to 100). In some, even in only the 5 years since 2000, the rise in school student spending was very marked, with the index reaching 139 in the

Czech Republic, 158 in Hungary, 147 in Ireland, 152 in Korea, and 147 in the Slovak Republic. In only Belgium was the recent level lower than in 2000 (at 96).

📖 *Education at a Glance: OECD Indicators – 2008 Edition*, Chapter B.

Classes are larger in lower secondary compared with in primary schools (on average, nearly three students more per class), alongside marked differences between countries with big and small classes: Lower secondary average class sizes of 30 or more in Korea, Japan, Brazil, Chile, and Israel contrast sharply with Iceland, Luxembourg, Switzerland and the Russian Federation where both primary and lower secondary classes are, on average, at or below 20 students per class. Primary school classes (21.5 per class OECD average) are generally smaller than in lower secondary schools (24.0 per class). Switzerland and the United Kingdom are minor exceptions to the "primary school classes are smaller" finding.

📖 *Education at a Glance: OECD Indicators – 2008 Edition*, Chapter D.

The investments made in teachers, as indicated by teacher salary levels, have gone up in real terms over the past decade in most countries: Teachers' salaries have risen in real terms in both primary and secondary education in most of the countries for which OECD has trends data (comparing 1996 and 2006 in 19 systems covering 17 countries). The biggest increases – approximately doubling – have taken place in Hungary. How large have been the increases depends in part on position on the salary scale. Starting salaries have risen faster than mid-career or top-of-the-scale levels, for instance, in Australia, Denmark, England, and Scotland. Largely static or even falling salary levels are only found – but note that not all countries supply data on teacher salaries – for the experienced teachers in Australia, starting secondary teachers in French Belgium, and starting primary teachers and those with 15 years experience in Switzerland, but more noticeable teacher salary decreases have been seen in Spain.

📖 *Education at a Glance: OECD Indicators – 2008 Edition*, Chapter D.

Some countries use a "career-based" model of teacher employment which brings its own strengths, weaknesses, and policy implications … In "career-based" systems, teachers expect to stay long in the public service after early entry and once recruited are allocated to posts according to internal rules (*e.g.* France, Japan, Korea and Spain). These systems tend to avoid problems of teacher shortages but there are real concerns about how far teacher education is connected to school and student needs, with lack of incentives for continued professional development and of responsiveness to local needs.

… Others have "position-based" systems, with their own strengths and weaknesses: These systems tend to select the "best" candidate for each position, whether by external recruitment or internal promotion, with wider access to the

Figure 2.1. **Spending per school student going up**

Change in the number of students in expenditure on educational institutions, and in expenditure per "school" student (2000, 2005) (2000 = 100, 2005 constant prices)

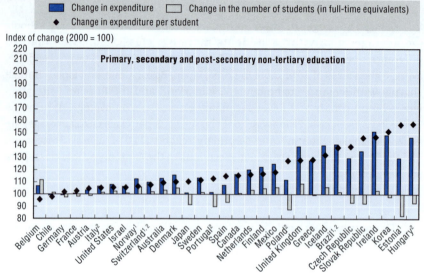

1. Public expenditure only.
2. Public institutions only.

Source: OECD (2008), *Education at a Glance: OECD Indicators – 2008 Edition*, OECD Publishing, Paris.

StatLink http://dx.doi.org/10.1787/401862824252

profession in terms of age or previous career experience (*e.g.* Canada, Sweden, Switzerland, and the United Kingdom). The problems typically encountered in these systems are shortages, especially in mathematics, sciences, etc., difficulties in ensuring a core of good teachers beyond age 40, and greater disparities in teacher quality between attractive and unattractive districts/schools.

📖 *Teachers Matter: Attracting, Developing and Retaining Effective Teachers*, 2005, Executive Summary.

Teacher aspirations can be advanced by capitalising on their intrinsic motivations while making appropriate use of extrinsic motivators: Teachers are much more motivated by intrinsic rewards to enter but extrinsic factors become more important for practising teachers. The evidence suggests that people enter teaching to help young people to learn and other educational reasons, with material factors and working conditions becoming more important later on. Policies to meet teacher aspirations and enhance their motivation as professionals need to capitalise on the intrinsic factors, make appropriate use of extrinsic motivators, and ensure that teachers have good working conditions so that their motivation is maintained.

📖 *Education Policy Analysis – 2006 Edition*, Chapter 3.

Figure 2.2. **Total number of intended instruction hours in public institutions between the ages of 7 and 14 (2006)**

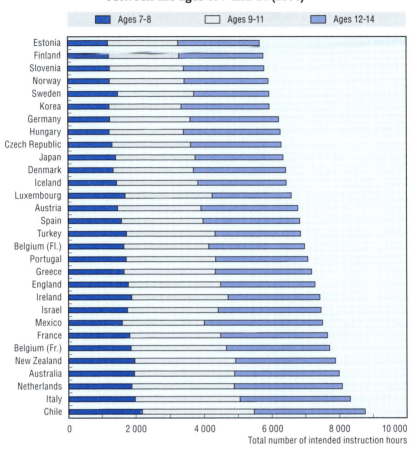

Source: OECD (2008), *Education at a Glance: OECD Indicators – 2008 Edition*, OECD Publishing, Paris.

StatLink http://dx.doi.org/10.1787/402183135853

Finland, as well as excelling in the PISA tests, is the OECD country with the lowest number of "intended instruction hours" for 7-14-year-olds, less than 70% of the accumulated hours in Italy: The average for OECD countries in "intended instruction hours" added up from requirements regarding pupils aged 7 years up to 14-year-old students is 6 907 hours. Requirements vary very widely, from 5 752 in Finland to 8 316 in Italy. The range is even greater when partner countries Estonia and Chile are included as in the former this stands at only 5 644 hours compared with 8 752 hours in Chile (Estonia is thus less than two-thirds of the Chilean teaching hours). This covers the compulsory and non-compulsory time when schools must offer teaching to school students, though actual hours may vary from this and there may be significant variations according to region or type of school.

📖 *Education at a Glance: OECD Indicators – 2008 Edition*, Chapter D.

School leadership is pivotal for the quality of schooling through creating the right organisational and educational conditions for effectiveness and improvement: A large body of research evidence on school effectiveness and improvement consistently highlights the pivotal role of leadership. It is nevertheless a complex role as leaders largely work outside the classrooms where the teaching and learning takes place. Hence, instead of shaping quality directly, leaders do so by creating the right conditions for good teaching and learning through such factors as professional motivations, capacities, and working environments. They are especially influential as regards four key dimensions: improving teacher quality; goal-setting, assessment and accountability; strategic resource management; and collaboration with external partners.

📖 *Improving School Leadership – Volume 1: Policy and Practice*, 2008, Chapter 1.

There has been very rapid recent investment in ICT for schools across OECD countries: That PISA surveys have taken place at regular intervals gives one way of showing the very rapid way in which ICT has been penetrating schools in OECD countries. The availability of computers in schools had at least doubled almost everywhere in only the three years up to 2003. In Greece, Portugal and Mexico, where very few computers were available for 15-year-old students in 2000, investments grew by a factor of five or more. For example, in Mexico, the number of students per computer fell from 81 to 12 over the period, and in Greece it fell from 58 to 12. Even in countries where the number of students per computer was already low in 2000, they halved again during this short period.

📖 *Education Policy Analysis – 2004 Edition*, Chapter 2.

It is necessary to reach thresholds of investments in ICT and in the skills and educational organisation to use them so as to reap educational benefits: Only in a certain relatively small number of countries have the thresholds of equipment and investment begun to be reached (at the time the chapter was written this included some of the Nordic countries, Australia, Hungary, Korea, New Zealand, the United Kingdom, and the United States) to allow most students to gain access to the technology and to use it frequently. Data from PISA 2003 show that even in countries with among the highest levels of investment in ICT in schools, often it is not used for much of the time. In the systems that have reached the thresholds, investment in equipment has often been complemented by extensive teacher training, and patterns of computer use by young people, both within the school and outside it, more often are for clearly educational and learning purposes.

📖 *Education Policy Analysis – 2004 Edition*, Chapter 2.

Some countries persist with repetition of school years as common practice despite its cost – to individuals and the system alike: In some school systems (France, Luxembourg and Spain), up to one-quarter of lower secondary school students repeat a year at some point, as do over 20% of primary pupils in the Netherlands and Mexico. But this is not the common situation across OECD countries. Although year repetition is often popular with teachers, there is little evidence that children gain benefit from it. Repetition is expensive – the full economic cost is up to USD 20 000 equivalent for each student who repeats a year – and schools have few incentives to take into account the costs involved.

📖 *No More Failures: Ten Steps to Equity in Education*, 2007, Chapter 4.

Formative assessment is among the most effective classroom strategies for promoting high student performance: Formative assessment differs from summative assessment (standardised tests, exams) in that the information gathered in the formative process is used on an on-going and targeted basis to shape improvements rather than the assessment serving as a summary of performance for wider purposes. The principles of formative assessment may be applied at the classroom and school [and even higher] levels to identify areas for improvement and to promote constructive cultures of evaluation. Meta-analyses show it is one of the most effective strategies for promoting high student performance. It is also important for improving equity and developing "learning to learn" skills.

📖 *Formative Assessment: Improving Learning in Secondary Classrooms*, 2005, Chapter 1.

Students are generally positive about school as a place, with younger and more successful students and girls the more positive: The evidence on student attitudes, from diverse international and national sources, reveals several general tendencies on reported satisfaction: students are fairly satisfied with school in general, although older students less than younger ones; students in higher tracks are more positive than students in lower tracks; girls tend to be more positive about school than boys. Countries where the measured sense of belonging is lowest among 15-year-olds are the Czech Republic, France, Belgium and Japan, and especially Korea and Poland. The cases of Japan and Korea show that low engagement can go hand-in-hand with high achievement. Countries where engagement is highest are Sweden, Ireland, Hungary and the United Kingdom.

📖 *Student Engagement at School: A Sense of Belonging and Participation. Results from PISA 2000, 2003; Demand-sensitive Schooling? Evidence and Issues*, 2006.

Anxiety towards mathematics is widespread: Taking the OECD countries as a whole, half of 15-year-old males and more than 6 in 10 female students report that they often worry that they will find classes in maths difficult and that they will get poor marks or grades. Nearly a third of all students across OECD countries agree that they get very nervous, tense and even helpless when doing mathematics problems or homework. Anxiety levels are highest in France, Italy, Japan, Korea, Mexico, Spain and Turkey, and are lowest in Denmark, Finland, the Netherlands, and Sweden. There is no obvious relationship between levels of anxiety and overall performance: countries with very high performance are sometimes those with the highest reported anxiety levels (Japan, Korea) and are sometimes those with the lowest anxiety (Finland, the Netherlands), though of course the anxious and the high-scoring students are not necessarily the same persons.

📖 *Learning for Tomorrow's World: First Results from PISA 2003, 2004, Chapter 3.*

Intrinsic interest in mathematics among students is far lower than it is in reading: Comparing PISA 2003, rich in mathematics data, with PISA 2000 which was rich in reading data, shows how much lower is interest in mathematics among 15-year-olds. About half across OECD countries agree that they are interested in the things they learn in their maths lessons, but less than 40% are ready to agree that they do mathematics because they enjoy it. Less than a third look forward to their mathematics classes.

📖 *Learning for Tomorrow's World: First Results from PISA 2003, 2004, Chapter 3.*

Immigrant students are motivated learners and have positive attitudes towards school: Immigrant students report similar or even higher levels of positive learning dispositions compared with their native peers. First and second generation students often report higher levels of interest and motivation in mathematics and more positive attitudes towards schooling, and in none of the countries do immigrant students report lower levels on these engagement and interest indicators. The consistency of this finding is striking given that there are substantial differences between countries in terms of immigrant populations, policies and histories, as well as immigrant student performance in PISA 2003.

📖 *Where Immigrant Students Succeed: A Comparative Review of Performance and Engagement in PISA 2003, 2006, Chapter 4.*

The closer parents are to schooling provision the more satisfied they tend to be about its achievements: Parents tend to be more satisfied with their own children's school than with the state of education in general; parents with children in school more satisfied than other parents; those involved in school governance more than other parents; women – who tend to be more active in their children's education and the life of the school – more than men. In evidence from diverse national studies, there is a generally positive level of reported satisfaction with schools by parents and the public. Education appears to be a high public priority alongside health and higher than many other calls on the public purse.

📖 *Demand-sensitive Schooling? Evidence and Issues*, 2006, Chapter 2.

2.2. Orientations for policy

Teacher employment and deployment are organised along markedly different lines in different systems: in some this follows a "career-based" model; in others, a "position-based" model. OECD analysis proposes the following directions to inform policy development whichever of the two applies:

- **Emphasise teacher quality over teacher quantity:** There is substantial research indicating that the quality of teachers and their teaching is the most important factor shaping student outcomes that is open to significant policy influence. Key ingredients in the teacher quality agenda include more attention to the criteria for selection into initial teacher education and teaching employment, on-going evaluation throughout the teaching career to identify areas for improvement, and recognising and rewarding effective teaching.

- **Develop teacher profiles to align teacher development and performance with school needs:** Countries need to have clear, concise statements of what teachers are expected to know and be able to do; these need to be embedded throughout the school and teacher education systems. The teacher profiles should encompass strong subject matter knowledge, pedagogical skills, the capacity to work effectively with a wide range of students and colleagues, to contribute to the school and the profession, and the capacity to continue developing.

- **View teacher development as a continuum:** The stages of initial teacher education, induction and professional development need to be well connected to create a coherent learning and development system for teachers – which they tend not to be in most countries. Lifelong learning for teachers implies supporting them more effectively in the early career stages and then providing incentives and resources for ongoing professional development.

- **Make teacher education and entry more flexible:** Provide more routes into the profession including: post-graduate study following an initial qualification in a subject matter field; para-professionals and teacher's aides given opportunities to gain full qualifications; and mid-career changers able to combine reduced teaching loads and concurrent participation in teacher preparation.

- **Transform teaching into a knowledge-rich profession:** Teachers need to be active agents in analysing their own practice in the light of professional standards and their own students' learning. Teachers need to engage more actively with new knowledge, and with professional development focused on the evidence base of improved practice.

- **Provide schools with genuine responsibility for teacher personnel management:** The evidence suggests that too often the selection process is dominated by rules about qualifications and seniority that bear little relationship to the qualifications needed to be an effective teacher. The school is the key agency for student learning – and hence for teacher selection, development, etc. – but will need highly-skilled leadership teams and support to carry this out.

📖 *Teachers Matter: Attracting, Developing and Retaining Effective Teachers*, 2005, Executive Summary.

OECD work on "formative assessment" (or "assessment for learning") – which is aimed at gearing teaching up to the needs and weaknesses of individuals in classroom environments – suggests a number of broad policy principles, some of which have much broader application:

- **Keep the focus on teaching and learning:** A constant for policy needs to be that, while it may seem obvious, the core of the education process lies in the teaching and learning which takes place every day in countless classrooms.

- **Align summative and formative assessment approaches:** Multiple measures of student progress are needed with a range of well-aligned assessments in order to improve validity, reliability and coherence. At the most basic level, "alignment" means to ensure that policies do not compete with each other; at a more sophisticated level, it means that the formative and summative evaluations reinforce each other.

- **Ensure that classroom, school, and system-level approaches to assessment are linked and are used formatively to shape improvement from top to bottom:** Policies that promote well-designed formative evaluations which are aligned – between what goes on in classrooms, in the schools in which the classes are located, and in their encompassing systems – will provide much clearer, coherent messages and help to ensure that systems are, at all levels, geared to improving learning.

- **Invest in training and support for formative assessment:** As teaching involving formative assessment calls for more advanced professional repertoires, it is natural that they need professional development – for student teachers, those just starting and the experienced. Policy can help with guidelines on implementation and by promoting exemplars of good practice.

- **Encourage innovation:** Policy makers and school leaders should promote innovation among confident teachers, and encourage peer support and involvement in research; policy can test research-based innovations through pilot projects.

- **Build good bridges between research, policy and practice:** Develop the research literacy of practitioners and officials, build best-practice databases, and promote new research in identified key areas where gaps exist.

- **Actively involve students and parents in the formative process:** As students are by definition interacting with teachers in the formative process, they need to be involved and encouraged to do so by setting and internalising their own learning goals and becoming skilled at peer- and self-assessment. The active involvement of parents as in other aspects of school life is always an advantage.

📖 *Formative Assessment: Improving Learning in Secondary Classrooms*, 2005, Chapter 6.

The quality of school leadership needs to be enhanced and it needs to be made sustainable. Four main policy levers, taken together, can improve school leadership practice:

- **Redefine school leadership responsibilities:** Leaders need to exercise a significant degree of autonomy if they are to influence quality and policy should ensure that they have this. Policy should encourage leaders to: support, evaluate and develop teacher quality; engage in goal-setting and organisational evaluation; enhance strategic financial and human resource management; and operate more widely than within the confines of the school itself.

- **Distribute school leadership:** Leadership is strengthened, not weakened, if the responsibilities of school principals are shared effectively with other middle management and school professionals and with school boards; policy should support and enable this to happen.

- **Develop skills for effective school leadership:** School leadership demands specific advanced competences that explicitly need development. Leadership development should contribute to the different career stages so policies should distinguish between preparation for leadership, induction programmes, and adequate in-service opportunities adapted to need and context. This career focus will also enhance attractiveness (next point).

- **Make school leadership an attractive profession:** Ensuring that the procedures for recruiting the key personnel of school leadership are highly professionalised is one important route to enhancing attractiveness. Another is to establish salaries at levels commensurate with workloads and responsibilities, compared with classroom teachers and those in other professions, and linked to local factors which influence attractiveness.

📖 *Improving School Leadership – Volume 1: Policy and Practice*, 2008, Executive Summary.

Strategies for transforming schools into "learning organisations" should include:

- **The reconsideration of teacher employment and working time regulations** in the light of demands for new teaching and learning skills and increased preparation time for the efficient use of digital technology. A similar reconsideration of student learning time is also needed.
- **Policies fostering school-based staff development** including activities in which teachers share their knowledge and experiences and co-operate in development projects.
- **Policies promoting networking** between teaching professionals and co-operation between other "learning organisations" including private companies.
- Move towards a **higher level of school autonomy in human resource management** and in the allocation of funds for ICT development.

📖 *Completing the Foundation for Lifelong Learning: An OECD Survey of Upper Secondary Schools*, 2004, Chapter 4.

Educational buildings and facilities need to accommodate both the known, identifiable needs of today and the uncertain demands of the future: Students need an environment that will support and enhance the learning process, encourage innovation, and be a tool for learning – these are much more important than creating a monument to aesthetics. Facilities need to be conceived not as an exclusive provision for the few, but as a resource to support lifelong education and recreation for all. They should provide good value for money. They should seek to minimise running and maintenance costs, ensuring that today's design decisions do not impose an unnecessary burden on future generations. Finally, they need to be designed to safeguard the well-being of the planet as well as the well-being of the individual.

📖 *Designs for Learning: 55 Exemplary Educational Facilities*, 2001, Introduction.

Programmes for seismic safety in schools should recognise the safety of children in schools as an important goal. The principles to guide such programmes to be established on an urgent basis to assure earthquake safety of new and existing schools should include:

- **Establish clear and measurable objectives for school seismic safety,** based on the level of risk and supported by the residents of communities in question and agencies at the local government level.
- **Define the level of the earthquake hazard** in order to facilitate the development and application of construction codes and standards.

- **Specify the desired ability of school buildings to resist earthquakes.** School buildings should be designed and constructed, or retrofitted, to prevent collapse, partial collapse or other failure that would endanger human life when subjected to specified levels of ground shaking and/or collateral seismic hazards.

- **Give priority to making new schools safe**. A longer timeframe will likely be needed to correct seismic weaknesses of existing school buildings.

📖 "OECD Recommendation Concerning Guidelines on Earthquake Safety in Schools", 2005.

ISBN 978-92-64-05989-4
Education Today
The OECD Perspective
© OECD 2009

Chapter 3

Transitions beyond Initial Education

OECD analyses have shed extensive light on the issues, arrangements, and policies surrounding the transitions beyond compulsory schooling. Extended education with at least completion of the upper secondary cycle is increasingly the norm right across the OECD countries. Alongside shared patterns are marked differences on such matters as the relative proportions who engage in general or vocational study, as well as the possibilities to combine education with employment. OECD studies on guidance, information systems and qualifications have shown that there is much scope for improving transitions. Vocational education and training have not been studied by OECD so extensively until recently and this is now being addressed. Policy orientations have stressed the need to improve the existence, diversity, relevance and transparency of different pathways, while protecting those left most vulnerable as others advance to further education and employment.

3.1. Key findings and conclusions

Secondary education has become the dominant experience for 17-year-olds in OECD countries: At age 17, over 8 in 10 young people in OECD countries are in secondary education (82%). In some it is the quasi-totality of the age group at 90% or more (Belgium, the Czech Republic, Finland, Germany, Hungary, Japan, Korea, Norway, Poland, the Slovak Republic, and Sweden). 17-year-olds in education are only the minority in Mexico (43%) and Turkey (34%). Not all countries have figures for 17-year-olds already in post-secondary non-tertiary education but among those that do, Austria stands out as having a sizeable minority of this teenage group (15%) transferred to such programmes. And in some countries, a small number have already launched on tertiary education even at this young age (the highest proportions being in Australia [4%], Canada [7%], Greece [14%], Ireland [6%], the Netherlands [6%], New Zealand [4%], Turkey [6%], and the United States [4%]).

📖 *Education at a Glance: OECD Indicators – 2008 Edition*, Chapter C.

Nearly three-quarters of 18-year-olds are still in education across OECD countries (73%), with already over a fifth in post-secondary education: In certain countries, the large majority of the age group continues in secondary education at 18 years: 80-90% in the Czech Republic, Denmark, Germany, and Norway, and over 90% in Finland (93%), Poland (92%), and Sweden (93%). In others, significant numbers have already embarked on tertiary programmes – a third or more of the age band in Belgium (36%), Canada (36%), Ireland (34%), and the United States (40%), rising to two-thirds in Greece (69%) and Korea (66%). Over a quarter of Austrian and Irish 18-year-olds (both at 26%) are in non-tertiary post-secondary programmes.

📖 *Education at a Glance: OECD Indicators – 2008 Edition*, Chapter C.

Completion of upper secondary education has become the norm over the past 20-30 years: Compared with more than three-quarters younger adults with upper secondary level education (78%), this stood at just under two-thirds for the older 45-54-year-olds in 2006 (65%) and just above half (55%) for the 55-64-year-olds. In certain countries, the increase in attainment between the younger and older adult cohorts separated by 30 years of age is dramatic: in Greece, it goes from 34% to 75%; in Spain, from 27% to 64%; and especially in Korea where it has exploded from 37% to a universal 97%.

📖 *Education at a Glance: OECD Indicators – 2008 Edition*, Chapter A.

For young adults across OECD countries, very nearly 7 years can now be expected to be spent in education between the ages of 15 and 29: Synthesising current enrolment patterns for young people in their latter teens and twenties, not far off half (6.7 years) of the 15 years between mid-teenage years and the end of their twenties will now be spent in education. Eight years or more of this age span is spent in education in Denmark, Finland (women), Germany (men), Iceland, the Netherlands (men), Poland (women), and Sweden (women). The "educational expectancy" of this transition age group tends to be longer among young women than young men though there are still exceptions to this (Australia, Austria, Germany, Japan, Mexico, the Netherlands, Switzerland, Turkey).
📖 *Education at a Glance: OECD Indicators – 2008 Edition*, Chapter C.

A relatively even balance between students enrolled in upper secondary general and vocational programmes across OECD as a whole hides very large differences across countries: Just over half of upper secondary level students (53.8%) are in "general" and the others are in pre-vocational and vocational tracks and those combining work with school. Over 65% are in "general" tracks in Canada, Greece, Hungary, Ireland, Japan, Korea, Mexico, Portugal and the United States. On the other hand, over 65% are in the vocational tracks in Austria, Belgium, the Czech Republic, Finland, the Netherlands, and the Slovak Republic.
📖 *Education at a Glance: OECD Indicators – 2008 Edition*, Chapter C.

The educational foundation – effective professionalised pedagogy and guidance – in vocational education and training (VET) programmes is often under-developed: Teaching vocational subjects requires special competence but, outside systems in the German tradition, pedagogical and teaching issues tend to be neglected. This is compounded by the perception of VET as "low status" which can impact on the quality of teacher recruits. Career guidance for job-bound, vocational careers is under-developed, in part because it is assumed that occupational choice is already clear. Attention to educational and vocational issues tends to be squeezed by the personal and social guidance needs of a minority of students with particular difficulties.
📖 *Education Policy Analysis – 2004 Edition*, Chapter 1; *Career Guidance and Public Policy: Bridging the Gap*, 2004, Chapter 3.

Certain countries do not mix education with employment together for young adults ... How the average 6.7 of the 15 years between 15 and 29 years will be experienced – in particular whether it will include being in employment status while also in education – varies sharply from country to country. There are some where these years will be primarily devoted to education without mixing this with employment status. For instance, less than 12 months on

Figure 3.1. **Completion of upper secondary education
is now the norm across OECD countries**

Population attaining at least upper secondary education (2005), percentage by age group

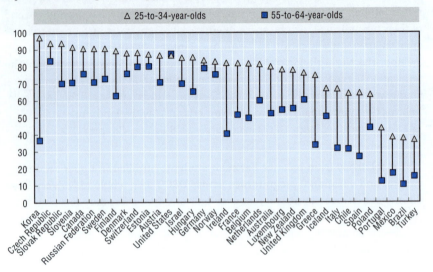

Note: Countries are in descending order left to right based on the percentage of the 25-to-34-year-olds having attained at least upper secondary education.

Source: OECD (2008), *Education at a Glance: OECD Indicators – 2008 Edition*, OECD Publishing, Paris.

StatLink ⟨🔗⟩ http://dx.doi.org/10.1787/401474646362

average from age 15 to 29 are counted as being in both education and employment (combining males and females) in the following countries: Belgium (0.5 in the total 6.5 years in education between these ages), Greece (0.3 in 6.3), Hungary (0.7 in 7.1), Ireland (0.9 in 5.2), Italy (0.5 in 6.4), Japan (0.7 in 5.7 up to the age of 24 years), Luxembourg (0.3 in 7.4), Portugal (0.6 in 5.9), the Slovak Republic (0.9 in 6.3), Spain (0.9 in 5.6), and Turkey (0.4 in 3.1).

... in others, being in "education" means being in employment as well for many young people: There are other countries with a "mixed model" where an important part of the years in education are counted as being simultaneously in employment, including on work study programmes. In some countries indeed, more than half of this time in education will have the double status combining it with employment (Australia, Denmark, Iceland [for women], the Netherlands, Switzerland, and the United Kingdom [for women]).

📖 *Education at a Glance: OECD Indicators – 2008 Edition*, Chapter C.

Across the OECD, 6.5% of 15-19-year-olds are not in education or employment, with more than double this level (14.6%) for 20-24-year-olds and significantly more in some countries: The countries where the shares of

Figure 3.2. **Expected years in education and not in education for 15-to-29-year-olds (2006)**

Division of the 15 years, by education, work and unemployment status

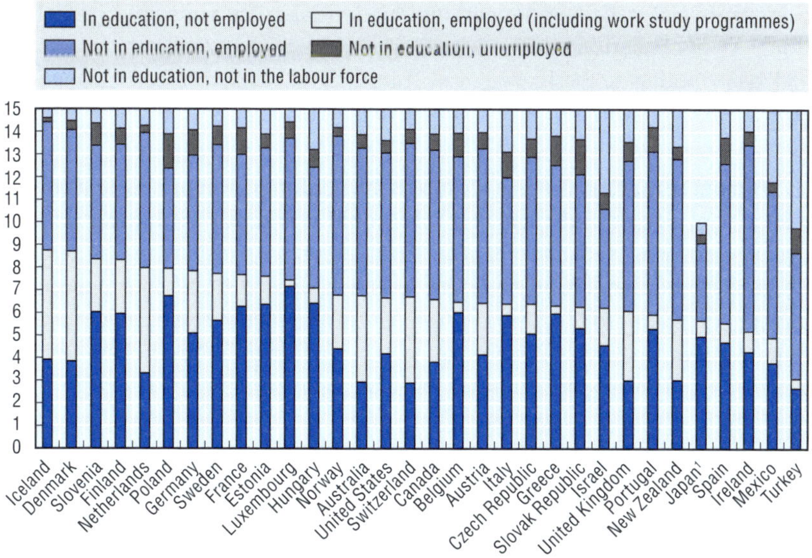

Note: Countries are ranked in descending order left to right according to expected years in education.
1. Data refer to 15-to-24-year-olds.
Source: OECD (2008), *Education at a Glance: OECD Indicators – 2008 Edition*, OECD Publishing, Paris.

StatLink http://dx.doi.org/10.1787/402165765880

the teenage group out of education and employment in 2006 reach double figures are Italy (11.8%), Mexico (17% in 2004), New Zealand (11.3%), Spain (10.1%), with a high 37.7% in Turkey in 2005. The numbers out of education and employment among adults in their early twenties tend to be significantly higher: more than 20% of the 20-24-year-olds are in this situation in Italy (22.8%), Mexico (27.4%, 2004), Poland (20.7%), and the Slovak Republic (22.8%), with very high levels (47.1%) in Turkey in 2005.

📖 *Education at a Glance: OECD Indicators – 2008 Edition*, Chapter C.

The problems faced by those who do not complete upper secondary education increase and are long lasting in countries where there are relatively fewer of them with this low attainment: A group of young people – defined for the OECD study as young adults aged 20-24 who do not have upper secondary education and are not currently in education – are facing difficult transitions from education to work and are at great risk of marginalisation. The numbers falling into this at-risk group varied from 4.6% in Norway in 2002 to as high as 48.8% in Portugal. A low level of education becomes a greater handicap as a country's global level of qualification goes up and as post-secondary education in different forms spreads among its population. What is worse, more experience – a longer potential presence on the labour market – does not make up for an initial deficit of educational credentials. The consequences of this initial lack of education may thus be long-lasting.

📖 *From Education to Work: A Difficult Transition for Young Adults with Low Levels of Education*, 2005, Chapter 2.

In most countries, there is a drop in the students at upper secondary level with special needs and receiving additional resources compared with the primary and lower secondary levels: For students with disabilities, a median of 1.6% receive additional funding at this level as against 3.3% for lower secondary. (The only exception to the drop between levels among the countries with data is England.) Similarly, the proportion getting additional financial resources specifically for learning difficulties is lower at the upper than the lower secondary level, again with the exception of England. For those recognised as having disadvantages and being thereby entitled to additional resources, there is again a drop between the two levels in most countries, with only the Slovak Republic showing a marginal increase from lower to upper secondary.

📖 *Students with Disabilities, Learning Difficulties and Disadvantages: Policies, Statistics and Indicators – 2007 Edition*, Chapter 4.

There is an important gap between the developed cognitive capacity in mid teenagers ("high horsepower") and their emotional maturity ("poor steering"): The insights provided by neuroscience on adolescence are especially important as this is the period when so much takes place in an individual's educational career. The secondary phase of education brings key decisions to be made with long-lasting consequences regarding personal, educational, and career options. At this time, young people are already well-developed in terms of cognitive capacity ("high horsepower") but they are immature ("poor steering"), not just because of inexperience but because of under-developed neurological emotional development.

📖 *Understanding the Brain: The Birth of a Learning Science*, 2007, "Conclusions and Future Prospects".

3.2. Orientations for policy

There are different ingredients for successful arrangements and systems, over and above a healthy economy, which may be more or less present and combine in different ways but which are all conducive to effective transition:

- **Well-organised pathways that connect initial education with work and further study:** The chances of solid transition outcomes are higher where young people have available learning pathways and qualifications frameworks that are clearly defined, well organised and open, designed and developed in a lifelong learning perspective, with effective connections to post-school destinations, whether work or further study.

- **Effective institutions and processes:** Countries with good transition outcomes are characterised by strong institutional frameworks to support the transition, normally developed over an extensive period. Such institutional frameworks appear to be most effective when they are able to combine central regulation with local flexibility.

- **Widespread opportunities to combine workplace experience with education:** Workplace experience combined with education can be important in order to: improve the quality of learning by making it more applied and relevant; develop important work-related knowledge and skills; have a positive impact on the firm as a learning organisation.

- **Good information and guidance:** Good information and guidance become increasingly important as the education and employment choices that face young people change and become more complex. This in turn calls for approaches that place much more emphasis on active career planning and development rather than "matching" to particular jobs or programmes.

- **Tightly-knit safety nets for those at risk:** High rates of upper secondary completion and achievement are important in reducing the numbers at risk and in reducing disparities between social groups; they are also important in making safety nets more affordable for those who do drop out of school.

📖 *From Initial Education to Working Life: Making Transitions Work*, 2000, Chapter 4.

The lifelong learning approach entails a broad conception of foundation learning at the end of the secondary cycle: Most countries report reforms in this area that are aimed at raising the level of qualification of school-leavers and retaining more young people in upper secondary education. These include:

- **Increasing the relevance of initial education to work and the value of work-related qualifications in the job market:** This general aim to create a better match between the objectives of education systems and the needs of the firm can be done in various ways, including, for instance, the broadening and development of new frameworks for vocational education for young people in schools (as in Australia) or through reinforcing collaboration between the different partners (as in the reform of the dual system in French-speaking Belgium).

- **Broadening criteria for reforming school qualifications:** Looking beyond particular knowledge or competence sets, reforms include the recognition of prior learning (*e.g.* Australia); recognition of achievement across a whole programme rather than specific subject attainment (*e.g.* Ireland); the development of a national certificate using "achievement standards" developed for the school curriculum and unit standards from the national qualifications framework (*e.g.* New Zealand).

- **Developing better progression routes for young people within and between qualifications:** Examples include enabling the easier vertical and horizontal transfer from one educational level to another (Slovenia) and flexible dual trajectories combining learning and work (the Netherlands).

📖 *Qualifications Systems: Bridges to Lifelong Learning*, 2007, Chapter 2.

Enhance the leadership capacity and function of guidance services as well as co-ordination between education and employment: Current mechanisms for leadership and co-ordination are generally weak though being tackled in some places (such as Luxembourg, Norway and the United Kingdom). Governments can provide strategic leadership, exercising this in partnership with other stakeholders: education and training providers, employers, trade unions, community agencies, students, parents, consumers, and career guidance practitioners. Strong co-operation between education and employment portfolios is particularly important so as to integrate educational and occupational information and to include a strong labour market perspective in schools' career guidance programmes.

📖 *Career Guidance and Public Policy: Bridging the Gap*, 2004, Chapter 9

Recognise the gap between the cognitive capacity and emotional maturity in teenagers to avoid definitive choices: The gap between intellectual and emotional capacity cannot imply that important choices should simply be delayed until adulthood when the gap closes. It does suggest, with the additional powerful weight of neurological evidence, that the options taken should not take the form of definitively closing doors.

📖 *Understanding the Brain: The Birth of a Learning Science*, 2007, Chapter 2.

ISBN 978-92-64-05989-4
Education Today
The OECD Perspective
© OECD 2009

Chapter 4

Higher Education

Countries share a very rapid expansion of higher or tertiary education which means that instead of this being an experience enjoyed by a privileged minority it has now become even the majority experience of each new cohort. There are other broad trends visible across the OECD – for instance, the growing international tertiary education market and the greater formalisation of quality assurance. There has been prominent OECD work on higher education latterly, with the Guidelines for Quality Provision in Cross-border Higher Education, a major review of tertiary education, and new work underway on assessment of higher education outcomes (AHELO). OECD policy orientations have included acceptance that students should contribute to the costs of their study (with appropriate safeguards), the need to develop e-learning and guidance systems, and reinforcement of the regional and innovation role of higher education institutions (HEIs).

4.1. Key findings and conclusions

Many more young adults are now in education even compared with a decade ago, accounting for a quarter of 20-29-year-olds and with university programme entry up more than 20 percentage points: An average of one quarter of young adults aged 20-29 are enrolled in education across OECD countries, and 30% or more are in Australia, Denmark, Finland, Greece, Iceland, Norway, Poland, and Sweden, and in the partner economy Slovenia. In contrast, only Denmark had 30% of 20- to 29-year-olds enrolled in education in 1995. Enrolment among 20-29-year-olds doubled or more since then in the Czech Republic, Greece, and Hungary. Entry rates to tertiary-type A education went up by more than 20 percentage points across the OECD since 1995, and by more than 15 points since 2000 in Australia, the Czech Republic, Greece, Italy, the Slovak Republic, and partner country Israel.

📖 *Education at a Glance: OECD Indicators – 2008 Edition*, Chapters A and C.

Figure 4.1. **Population that has attained at least tertiary education (2006)**
Percentage, by age group

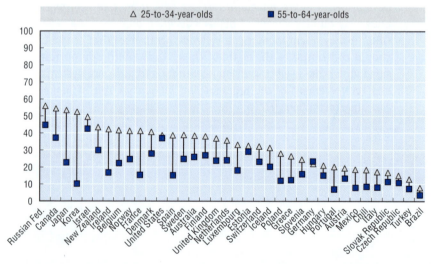

Source: OECD (2008), *Education at a Glance: OECD Indicators – 2008 Edition*, OECD Publishing, Paris.

StatLink 🔗 http://dx.doi.org/10.1787/401474646362

EDUCATION TODAY: THE OECD PERSPECTIVE – ISBN 978-92-64-05989-4 – © OECD 2009

Over half the population of OECD countries will participate in tertiary education at some stage of their lives based on current patterns of entry: Participation rates of tertiary education of over 50% for a single age cohort are becoming the benchmark for OECD countries. (This refers to "net entry rates" which are calculated as the proportion in a synthetic age cohort who go into tertiary education at some point in their lives based on current enrolment patterns.) For some countries in 2006, such entry rates are substantially higher again: over 70% can expect to enter university-type programmes (tertiary A) in Australia, Finland, Iceland, New Zealand, Poland, and Sweden. Other countries – Denmark, Greece, Israel, Korea, the Russian Federation, Slovenia, and the United Kingdom – reach levels of 80% combining net entry rates in university-type programmes and non-university type programmes.

📖 *Tertiary Education for the Knowledge Society: Volume 1*, 2008, Chapter 2; *Education at a Glance: OECD Indicators – 2008 Edition*, Chapter C.

Nearly a third of university students fail to graduate and such "dropout" is higher still in non-university tertiary programmes: On average across the 24 OECD countries for which data are available, 31% of university (tertiary type A) students fail to successfully complete the programmes they undertake. Survival rates differ widely. The countries where over three-quarters of university students complete the programme are Japan (91%), Denmark (81%), the United Kingdom (79%), Germany (77%), Flemish Belgium and the Netherlands (76%). In contrast, in Hungary, Italy, New Zealand and the United States less that 6 in 10 of those who enter go on to complete. The non-completion rate in vocational, non-university programmes stands even higher than in university-type programmes at 38%, and is highest in New Zealand, Sweden and the United States at around two-thirds.

📖 *Education at a Glance: OECD Indicators – 2008 Edition*, Chapter A.

Just over a quarter of expenditure on educational institutions across the OECD is accounted for by tertiary education: Large differences between countries in the size of systems, pathways available to students, programme durations and the organisation of teaching, mean that there are large differences in the level of expenditure which countries spend on tertiary education. Korea and the United States spend 2.4% and 2.9% of their GDP respectively on higher education institutions – the highest among OECD countries – but far less than this from the public purse as these two countries are also those with the highest proportion of private expenditure. (In the case of Korea, the 2.4% figure is made up of 0.6% public and 1.8% private). Australia, Canada, Denmark, Finland, Poland, Sweden, and partner economy Chile also show high overall levels, at 1.6% or more of GDP.

📖 *Education at a Glance: OECD Indicators – 2008 Edition*, Chapter B.

Whether tertiary education is treated as a public or private good varies considerably across countries, including the extent of public subsidy to students and their households: There are no tuition fees charged in university-type tertiary education in the five Nordic countries, the Czech Republic, Ireland, and Poland. In contrast, in the United States, tuition fees for nationals in public institutions reach more than USD 5 000. Most OECD and partner countries charge higher fees in private institutions; Finland and Sweden are the only countries with no fees in either public or private institutions. An OECD average 18% of public spending on tertiary education is devoted to supporting students, households and other private entities, and this rises to a quarter or more in Denmark, the Netherlands, Sweden, and the United Kingdom, a third in Australia, and over 40% in New Zealand, Norway and Chile. It is less than 10% in the Czech Republic, France, Greece, Korea, Mexico, Poland, Portugal, Spain, and Switzerland.

📖 *Education at a Glance: OECD Indicators – 2008 Edition*, Chapter B.

OECD analysis has identified five groups of countries in their approach to assisting students financially: Of the countries participating in the OECD Tertiary Education Review, first there are those which base their student support exclusively on a public loan fund without grants (Iceland and Norway). A second group – Australia, Japan, the Netherlands, New Zealand, Sweden, and the United Kingdom – combines a public loan system with a publicly-funded grant scheme. A third group – Estonia, Finland, Poland, and Portugal – is like the second except that the loans are provided by commercial banks with public subsidy and/or public guarantee. A fourth group of countries – Chile, China, and Korea – offers a wide choice of schemes through a mix of a public loan fund, commercial banks, and grants. A fifth group – the Flemish Community of Belgium, Croatia, the Czech Republic, Greece, Mexico, the Russian Federation, Spain, and Switzerland – has no loan scheme and bases student support on grants.

📖 *Tertiary Education for the Knowledge Society: Volume 1, 2008*, Chapter 4.

OECD countries share the trend of moving to more highly developed and sophisticated quality assurance systems in higher education: Increased autonomy over a wide range of institutional operations has gone hand-in-hand with more sophisticated quality assurance based on national quality agencies. At the beginning of the 1990s such agencies existed in only a handful of countries; by the end of the decade they had been established in almost all of them. This has shifted responsibility for quality assessment from being a mainly internal judgement by institutions themselves to an external process by the national agencies and by peer review and funding bodies.

📖 *Education Policy Analysis – 2003 Edition*, Chapter 3.

There has been a fourfold increase in foreign students since the mid-1970s, highly concentrated in a small number of destination countries: In the 1990s, there was a sharp increase in cross-border higher education – the international mobility of students and teachers, educational programmes and higher education institutions – which has continued since. The number of foreign students worldwide stood at around 0.6 million in 1975 and has now risen to an estimated 2.9 million by 2006. The mobility of students alone was estimated as worth more than USD 40 billion in export income in 2004. Foreign students are highly concentrated in a few countries. Two-thirds of them are studying in only seven destination countries: nearly half (49%) attend higher education in the top four destination countries (the United States, the United Kingdom, Germany and France), with another 16% accounted for by the next three (Australia [6.3%], Canada [5.1%], and Japan [4.4%]).

📖 Education at a Glance: OECD Indicators – 2008 Edition, Chapter C; Education Policy Analysis – 2006 Edition, Chapter 2.

Figure 4.2. **Distribution of foreign students in tertiary education, by country of destination (2006)**

Percentage of foreign tertiary students reported to the OECD who are enrolled in each country of destination

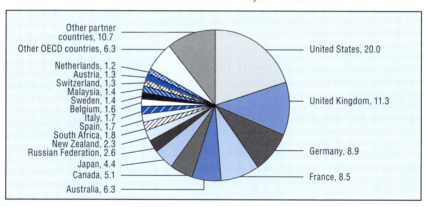

Source: OECD (2008), Education at a Glance: OECD Indicators – 2008 Edition, OECD Publishing, Paris.

StatLink ᵃᵢₛ⧳ http://dx.doi.org/10.1787/402158641726

An internationalisation policy centred on importing higher education is more appropriate for many countries which cannot afford to base policies on exporting higher education: The benefits to a country of a developed international policy are especially obvious in those countries which are net "exporters". They include the "skilled migration" benefits of attracting talented students and academics to promote the knowledge economy and the "revenue-generating" benefits of advancing human capital investment using income from foreign students' fees. The "capacity-building" benefits, on the other hand, stem from the use of imported higher education as a relatively quick way to build an emerging country's capacity, and this has proved particularly effective in several Asian and Middle Eastern countries.

📖 *Education Policy Analysis – 2006 Edition*, Chapter 2.

E-learning has not yet revolutionised learning and teaching in higher education systems: The current immaturity of on-line learning is demonstrated by low adoption of content management systems. This refers to electronic content being split into "learning objects", to be manipulated and reconstituted for multiple pedagogic purposes: only 6.6% of those responding to the UK-based Observatory on Borderless Higher Education (OBHE) survey of 122 Commonwealth institutions reported institution-wide adoption in 2004. ICT has had more impact on administrative services than on the fundamentals of teaching and learning.

📖 *E-learning in Tertiary Education: Where do We Stand?*, 2005, Conclusion; *Policy Brief*, 2006.

Career guidance has generally not caught up with the changing face of tertiary education: The changing situation in tertiary education – expanded participation, increased diversity, choice and competition – poses major challenges for career guidance that few countries seem well equipped to handle. At this level, such services tend to be limited both in scale and in focus, and inconsistent in quality. Ireland and the United Kingdom are two examples where comprehensive tertiary services have been developed and it is being addressed elsewhere.

📖 *Career Guidance and Public Policy: Bridging the Gap*, 2004, Chapter 3.

Higher numbers of young science graduates reflect both larger total graduate numbers and student choices, with smaller gender differences in science graduation tending to go along with fewer science graduates overall: The countries with higher than the OECD average of 1 694 science graduates per 100 000 25-34-year-olds are: Australia, Finland, France, Ireland, Korea, New Zealand, Poland, Sweden, Switzerland, and the United Kingdom. In the highest, Korea at 3 863, the male science graduates far outnumber the females by 4 735 to 2 596 (35% female). The smallest gender differences are found in Iceland (45% female), Italy (45%), Mexico (45%), Poland (45%), the Slovak Republic (43%), and indeed in Turkey (57%) where there are more women science graduates per young population than men. The contrast with Korea is clear, and the contrast is found also with Ireland (33% females) and France (32%), and it is even greater in Switzerland (21%) and Japan (20%).

📖 *Education at a Glance: OECD Indicators – 2008 Edition*, Chapter A.

44

The participation of students with special needs in higher education is increasing, sometimes markedly: In the United Kingdom, for instance, the number of students with a disability increased from 2% of the higher education student population to 5.3% between 1994 and 2003 while in France the equivalent number increased tenfold from the early 1980s. Countries with a medical approach to defining disability (*e.g.* France, Germany) tend to have more students with impairments or long-tem illnesses at higher education while those following a needs-based approach (*e.g.* Canada, United Kingdom) tend to enrol more students with learning difficulties.

📖 *Disability in Higher Education*, 2004.

Despite the major demographic changes taking place in OECD countries, the evolution of the academic workforce is not primarily a reflection of these wider demographic trends: The age pyramid of academic staff reflects less the ageing of populations in general, and more an employment system in higher education whose hallmark is permanence with efforts to maintain relatively fixed student-teacher ratios. Similarly, the changing composition of academic staff reflects less general demographic developments and more the diversification of the profession and the restructuring of relationships between academics and their institutions.

📖 *Higher Education to 2030 – Volume 1: Demography*, 2008, Chapters 3 and 4.

4.2. Orientations for policy

While recognising differences of culture and approach in national tertiary education systems, there is a number of common main elements that underpin sound planning and policy-making:

- **Develop and articulate a vision for tertiary education:** Countries should as a priority develop a comprehensive and coherent vision for the future of tertiary education, to guide the medium- and long-term in harmony with national social and economic objectives. Ideally, it should result from a systematic review and entail a clear statement of strategic aims.

- **Establish sound instruments for steering towards and implementing that vision:** Tertiary education authorities need to develop their review and monitoring capacity for the system as a whole as opposed to the standard instruments of institutional administration. Within the overall vision, steering instruments need to establish a balance between institutional autonomy and public accountability. Allowing the play of student choice can help to improve quality and efficiency.

- **Strengthen the ability of institutions to align with the national tertiary education strategy:** Institutions should be encouraged to develop an outward focus, including via external representation on their governing bodies, and be required to establish strategic plans. The national policy framework should give institutions the means effectively to manage their wider responsibilities.

📖 *Tertiary Education for the Knowledge Society: Volume 1, 2008, Chapter 3.*

Lessons drawn from OECD review about the implementation of tertiary education reforms suggest that they should:

- **Recognise the different viewpoints of stakeholders** through iterative policy development.
- **Allow for bottom-up initiatives** to come forward as proposals by independent committees.
- **Establish *ad-hoc* independent committees** to initiate tertiary education reforms and involve stakeholders.
- **Use pilots and experimentation**.
- **Favour incremental reforms** over comprehensive overhauls unless there is wide public support for change.
- **Avoid reforms with concentrated costs and diffused benefits**.
- **Identify potential losers** from tertiary education reform and build in compensatory mechanisms.
- **Create conditions for and support the successful implementation of reforms**.
- **Ensure communication about the benefits of reform and the costs of inaction**.
- **Implement the full package of policy proposals**.

📖 *Tertiary Education for the Knowledge Society: Volume 2, 2008, Chapter 11.*

Among the principles and pointers for quality assurance in tertiary education, in addition to the general requisites of building the focus on student outcomes and the capacity for quality assurance, are:

- **Design a quality assurance framework consistent with the goals of tertiary education, and ensure that quality assurance serves both improvement and accountability purposes.**
- **Combine internal and external quality assurance mechanisms**.
- **Make stakeholders such as students, graduates and employers visible in the evaluation procedures.**
- **Enhance the international comparability of the quality assurance framework**.

📖 *Tertiary Education for the Knowledge Society: Volume 1, 2008, Chapter 5.*

Graduates should contribute to the costs of study so as to increase resources for higher education, with safeguards to support students from poorer backgrounds: A large and growing body of international evidence suggests that individuals who gain higher education qualifications enjoy substantial private benefit. There are important efficiency gains to be made in increasing the share of non-public sources of funding where these are low, though the equity concerns are real. The change in the proportion of public *versus* private funding will not itself produce inequity so long as adequate financing overall exists and concerted efforts are made to improve the accessibility of higher education.

📖 *Education Policy Analysis – 2006 Edition*, Athens Ministerial summary.

Among the main principles guiding funding strategies in tertiary education, beyond ensuring that they promote the wider goals and societal benefit, are:

- **Use cost-sharing between the State and students as the principle to shape the sector's funding:** This means, *inter alia*, providing public subsidies to tertiary education studies, regardless of the sector of provision. But, it also means charging tuition fees to students, especially if limited public funds would either ration the number of students, jeopardise levels of spending per student, or restrict financial support for disadvantaged groups.

- **Make institutional funding to teaching formula-driven:** The criteria for the distribution of funds to institutions need to be clear, using transparent formulae which shield allocation decisions from political pressures while tailoring incentives to shape institutional plans towards national goals.

- **Improve cost-effectiveness:** Inefficiencies should be addressed through such means as linking funding more closely to graduation rates, reducing public subsidies for those who stay too long in their studies; eliminating some duplicated programmes; rationalising low- or declining-enrolment programmes; increased use of shared facilities; and expanding student mobility across institutions.

- **Back the overall funding approach with a comprehensive student support system:** A mixed system of grants and loans assists students in covering tuition and living costs, alleviating excessive hours in paid work or disproportionate reliance on family support. In many countries student support needs to be expanded and diversified.

📖 *Tertiary Education for the Knowledge Society: Volume 1*, 2008, Chapter 4.

In the international market for higher education, the different stakeholders need to contribute to protect students from low-quality provision and disreputable providers: The OECD, in close co-operation with UNESCO, has published a set of international *Guidelines for Quality Provision in*

Cross-border Higher Education (2005) recommending actions for different stakeholders. For governments, it is recommended that they:

- Establish, or encourage the establishment of a comprehensive, fair and transparent system of registration or licensing for cross-border higher education providers wishing to operate in their territory.

- Establish, or encourage the establishment of a comprehensive capacity for reliable quality assurance and accreditation of cross-border higher education provision.

- Consult and co-ordinate amongst the various competent bodies for quality assurance and accreditation both nationally and internationally.

- Provide accurate, reliable and easily accessible information on the criteria and standards for registration, licensure, quality assurance and accreditation of cross-border higher education, their consequences on the funding of students, institutions or programmes where applicable, and their voluntary or mandatory nature.

- Consider becoming party to and contribute to the development and/or updating of the appropriate UNESCO regional conventions on recognition of qualifications and establish national information centres as stipulated by the conventions.

- Where appropriate develop or encourage bilateral or multilateral recognition agreements, facilitating the recognition or equivalence of each country's qualifications based on the procedures and criteria included in mutual agreements.

- Contribute to efforts to improve the accessibility at the international level of up-to-date, accurate and comprehensive information on recognised higher education institutions/providers.

Create an effective interface between innovation and higher education systems: Such an interface is essential in order to reap the benefits from public and private investments in research and to ensure the vitality and quality of higher education systems. Directions for creating such an interface include:

- **Improve knowledge diffusion rather than commercialisation via stronger intellectual property rights (IPRs):** Innovation is not only a discovery process to then be commercialised; R&D is often problem-solving along a pathway of innovation. The diffusion capabilities and support activities of tertiary education institutions may thus be as important as discovery processes and policy should consider methods and instruments to promote them.

- **Improve and widen channels of interaction and encourage inter-institutional collaboration:** Linkages between the tertiary education sector and other actors in the research and innovation system, such as firms and public research organisations, need to be actively developed to ensure effective knowledge diffusion. When programmes are designed, they need to consider in particular the engagement of small- and medium-sized enterprises from all technological sectors as they tend to be under-represented in such collaborations.

- **Foster mobility across the research and innovation system:** Inter-sectoral mobility is one of the main vehicles for knowledge diffusion; mobility between firms, tertiary education institutions and public research organisation should be actively promoted.

📖 *Education Policy Analysis – 2006 Edition*, Chapter 1; *Tertiary Education for the Knowledge Society: Volume 2*, 2008, Chapter 7.

Government has a key role to play in joining up a wide range of policies and creating supportive environments to promote the *regional role* of higher education institutions. These include to:

- **Create more "joined up" decision-making** (finance, education, science and technology, and industry ministries, etc.) to co-ordinate decisions on priorities and strategies in regional development.

- Make **regional engagement and its agenda for economic, social and cultural development explicit** in higher education legislation and mission strategies.

- **Develop indicators and monitor outcomes** to assess the impact of higher education institutions on regional performance and encourage their participation in regional governance structures.

- Provide a **supportive regulatory, tax and accountability environment** for university-enterprise co-operation.

Higher education institutions themselves should change so that what is now active regional engagement in particularly forward-looking and entrepreneurial institutions becomes more widespread across the sector.

📖 *Higher Education and Regions: Globally Competitive, Locally Engaged*, 2007, Chapter 9.

ISBN 978-92-64-05989-4
Education Today
The OECD Perspective
© OECD 2009

Chapter 5

Adult Education and Training – Participation and Provision

With agreement on the importance of lifelong learning in OECD and by countries, it is natural that adult participation in education and training has been a focus of statistical work and of programme and policy analysis. The international data show how, for many countries, participation in formal education remains a rare occurrence for older adults, with very wide differences between countries in engagement in non-formal organised learning. The Nordic countries are near the top of most comparisons of participation and engagement. The OECD has conducted international reviews – the most recent published in 2005 – bringing together the education and employment perspectives, of provision and policies for adult learning, with complementary studies on qualifications, ageing, and financing.

5.1. Key findings and conclusions

Over 1 in 20 adults aged 30-39 are enrolled full- or part-time in formal education in OECD countries, as are 1.4% of the 40+ age group: The 20-29-year-olds enrolled in education, while all are "adults", include many who are completing their initial cycles of education and training. For older adults, 5.7% of the 30-39 age population across OECD countries are enrolled in education, full- or part-time. It is significantly higher than this in certain countries, at more than 1 in 10 in Australia (13.8%), Finland (13.8%), Iceland (12.5%), New Zealand (12.3%), and Sweden (13.2%). Some countries are unable to make the corresponding calculations for the 40+ age group, but where they can, the highest levels of enrolment are found in Australia (5.9%), Belgium (3.7%), Finland (3.2%), Iceland (3.4%), New Zealand (5.1%), and Sweden (3.0%).

📖 *Education at a Glance: OECD Indicators – 2008 Edition*, Chapter C.

There are countries where to be enrolled in education as an older adult remains a rare occurrence: With an OECD average of just under 6% for adults in their thirties in formal education, there are naturally countries where the level is significantly lower. Those at half or less below the average enrolment rate for 30-39-year-olds, include: France (2.6%), Germany (2.5%), Greece (1.1%), Korea (2.1%), Luxembourg (0.8%), the Netherlands (2.7%), and Turkey (1.6%). Lack of data prevents a number of OECD countries from making the corresponding calculations for the 40+ age group; where they can do so, 0.5% or fewer of these mature adults are in full- or part-time education in Austria, the Czech Republic, Germany, Ireland, Italy, Korea, Luxembourg, Portugal, the Slovak Republic, Switzerland and Turkey.

📖 *Education at a Glance: OECD Indicators – 2008 Edition*, Chapter C.

The chances of a working-age adult participating in job-related non-formal education and training during a year is less than 1 in 5 (18%), is slightly higher for men, and much higher for tertiary graduates: Across the OECD as a whole (based on 22 countries in 2003), 18% of 25-64-year-olds participated in organised job-related learning outside the formal education system, with men having a slightly higher chance (19%) of doing so than women (17%). Adults who have been through tertiary education are much more likely to have been involved in such job-related learning during the year at nearly a third (31%), women tertiary graduates even more so (32%). Those with upper secondary attainment

Figure 5.1. **Adults enrolled in education (2006)**

Percentage of the populations aged 30-39 years and 40 and older enrolled in formal education

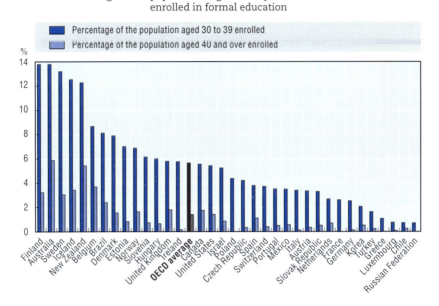

Source: OECD (2008), *Education at a Glance: OECD Indicators – 2008 Edition*, OECD Publishing, Paris.

StatLink http://dx.doi.org/10.1787/402156412821

are approximately at the same level on this indicator as the average for all people combined (17% compared with 18%). The very big drop is seen with working-age adults who have only been through schooling at the lower secondary level: for them, only 7% will do job-related organised learning during the year, and for women it is a mere 6%.

📖 *Education at a Glance: OECD Indicators – 2007 Edition*, Chapter C.

Adults are most likely to undertake job-related, non-formal education in three Nordic countries and the United States, plus France and Switzerland when the measure is lifetime training hours: Denmark (39%), Finland (36%), Sweden (40%), and the United States (37%) lead the way with a third or more of working-age adults participating in such learning in 2003 over the course of the preceding year. In all these cases, women are more likely to have done so than men, though in Denmark there is an even gender balance. Taking expected hours in training over the typical working life partly modifies the leading countries – Denmark, Finland and Sweden still feature but also Switzerland and France at over 600 lifetime hours, with Canada close behind. The advantage of tertiary graduates in job-related learning is clear, with their average expected hours exceeding 1 000 hours in Denmark, Finland, France, and Switzerland. Unlike the two Nordic countries, male graduates hold the advantage over females in France and, especially, Switzerland (1 422 hours for male as against 1 085 hours for female graduates).

📖 *Education at a Glance: OECD Indicators – 2007 Edition*, Chapter C.

Compared with the overall 18% of adults engaging in non-formal job-related training during the year, in 7 out of the 22 countries (with data) participation rates are at half of or below this OECD average: Engagement in organised non-formal, job-related learning remains a relatively infrequent matter in a number of OECD countries. Of the 22 supplying data, in 7 of them the participation rate during the previous year stood at 9% or less in Greece (4%), Hungary (4%), Italy (4%), the Netherlands (9%), Poland (9%), Portugal (7%), and Spain (6%). For tertiary graduates in two of these – Poland (29%) and Portugal (27%) – the rates was well above the overall OECD average combining all levels of educational background meaning that there are very wide gaps in training take-up between tertiary graduates and other workers; in the others, even tertiary graduates are below the 18% global average.

📖 *Education at a Glance: OECD Indicators – 2007 Edition*, Chapter C.

Surveys show that adults' participation in organised learning is consistently among the highest in the Nordic countries, and that participation declines with age and for the poorly qualified: Comparing national participation rates in adult learning as a whole is problematic because different surveys use different methodologies, time reference periods, and range of relevant learning experiences. Drawing on primarily European data (plus Korea and the United States) in 17 countries, country rankings give broadly similar results across different surveys. Denmark, Finland and Sweden rank highest in most, followed by the United Kingdom and Switzerland while Hungary, Portugal and Poland tend to be at the other end of the spectrum. Surveys find that education and adult learning are complementary and that the participation of 25-34-year-olds is often twice or more compared with 55-64-year-olds, and much more than this in countries where overall participation is lowest.

📖 *Promoting Adult Learning*, 2005, Chapter 1.

Insufficient opportunities for education are not the principal reason why many adults do not engage in learning: Evidence on barriers to participation suggests that under-investment in adult learning is due more to the demand side than to lack of supply of learning opportunities. Many adults are simply not interested. This can be because they are not aware of the need for training or because of lack of information, lack of incentives, or a perceived lack of returns. When asked about the obstacles, most refer to the key problem of lack of time, mainly due to work or family obligations (the opportunity costs). Lack of resources to pay for training is another key issue. The time required for training and the resulting opportunity costs could be reduced through more systematic recognition of acquired skills and competences, more efficient forms of training, individualised programmes of study, and more effective information and advice. Co-financing can help to share the time costs for training as well as the direct costs.

📖 *Promoting Adult Learning*, 2005, Chapter 5; *Co-financing Lifelong Learning: Towards a Systemic Approach*, 2004.

Brain research provides important additional support for adults' continued learning throughout the lifespan: One of the most powerful set of neurological findings on learning concerns the brain's remarkable properties of "plasticity" – to grow in response to experience and to prune itself when parts become unnecessary. This continues throughout the lifespan, and far further into old age than had previously been understood. The demands made on the individual and on his/her learning are key to the plasticity – the more one learns, the more one can learn. Neuroscience has shown that learning is a lifelong activity in which the more that it continues the more effective it is.

📖 *Understanding the Brain: The Birth of a Learning Science*, 2007, Chapter 2.

Brain research confirms the wider benefits of learning, especially for ageing populations: For older people, cognitive engagement, regular physical exercise, and an active social life promote learning and can delay degeneration of the ageing brain. The enormous and costly problems represented by ageing dementia in ever-ageing populations can be addressed through the learning interventions being identified through neuroscience. Combinations of improved diagnostics, opportunities to exercise, appropriate and validated pharmacological treatment, and good educational intervention can do much to maintain positive well-being and to prevent deterioration.

📖 *Understanding the Brain: The Birth of a Learning Science*, 2007, Chapter 2.

5.2. Orientations for policy

Developing and co-ordinating system-level policies for effective adult learning, especially engaging at-risk groups, means:

- **Developing adult learners at young ages:** This means considering as an entire portfolio the range of interventions to combat low adult attainment (training programmes, school-based policies, and earlier interventions). It means reducing the rate of dropout at school level and getting those young adults who do drop out of school back into second-chance opportunities as early as possible.

- **Working towards compatibility between training and employment:** In many countries, labour market programmes and the education system are independent, with few links to permit the training involved to count towards conventional qualifications. Linking the two can facilitate the move not just into work but into more solid careers.

- **Linking adult learning to social welfare programmes:** This is an integral aspect of active programmes – to shift away from passive welfare transfers towards training alternatives which strengthen labour market prospects. The linking of adult learning and welfare benefits policies is part of this trend.

- **Collaborating with the social partners:** Admitting the social partners into decision-making processes contributes to plans and policies concerning delivery methods, and to the recognition and certification of learning. The partners are key to qualification systems, and may be involved in actual delivery.

📖 *Promoting Adult Learning*, 2005, Chapter 5.

Shaping a coherent adult learning system requires adapted institutions for policy formulation and programme delivery and/or the setting of clear policy priorities and targets: Countries with high participation rates, such as the United Kingdom and some Nordic countries, have adopted either one or both approaches concurrently. Co-ordination institutions contribute through establishing priorities, defining appropriate financial incentives to increase adult participation, providing information and guidance, and improving the quality of provision through involving the different partners. Defining targets, on the other hand, can be an effective way of getting a diverse range of actors to work towards common goals.

📖 *Promoting Adult Learning*, 2005, Chapter 5.

Against the backdrop of the over-arching importance of lifelong learning, four key conclusions emerged from the 2003 OECD **co-financing lifelong learning policy** conference:

- Adequate financing of lifelong learning depends on **the creation of new institutional structures** to support financing schemes, **and a "whole of government"** approach to ensure that public authorities provide more systemic support for financing.

- **Financing schemes need to empower individual learners to choose** what, how, where and when to learn, and to enable them to exercise choice in deciding where to go with their acquired skills and competences.

- Lifelong learning must be **co-financed**, because government cannot shoulder the burden alone, and because the benefits of lifelong learning are widely shared; **government should concentrate its resources on those individuals least able to pay**.

● **Co-ordinated policy-making** by public authorities, and their collaboration with financial institutions, social partners and other stakeholders, are required in order to make further progress in the development and implementation of co-financing strategies.

📖 *Co-financing Lifelong Learning: Towards a Systemic Approach*, 2004, Chapter 3.

Co-financing is an underpinning principle for adult learners: There is considerable evidence that adult learning benefits adults themselves as well as employers and society. In order to minimise the risk of under-investment, many countries have experimented with co-financing savings and loan schemes that mirror the way benefits are shared. Matching individual contributions have been provided by the public authorities through individual grants or tax incentives, non-governmental organisations, and/or employers. Examples are found in many countries including Canada, the Netherlands, Spain, Switzerland, and the United Kingdom. It is an open question whether the resources provided really stimulate net new learning activity or whether they subsidise learning that would have occurred anyway.

📖 *Co-financing Lifelong Learning: Towards a Systemic Approach*, 2004, Chapter 2.

ISBN 978-92-64-05989-4
Education Today
The OECD Perspective
© OECD 2009

Chapter 6

Lifelong Learning

"Lifelong Learning" has been a defining goal for education and training policies for many years, emphasising the need for organised learning to take place over the whole lifespan and across the different main spheres that make up our lives ("life-wide"). OECD data confirm how extensive educational "careers" have become. There have been discrete studies which shed light on the nature of the challenge: the need to question the continued "front-end" expansion of education systems if lifelong learning is to be achieved; the room for considerable improvement in guidance systems; the importance of financing and qualification systems. Despite acknowledgement of its importance, holistic analyses of lifelong learning have been less a feature of OECD work in recent years and the relatively dated evidence base comparing countries in their implementation of this broad aim similarly underlines that implementation in countries is patchy and often disappointing.

6.1. Key findings and conclusions

OECD proposes four fundamental features of lifelong learning:

- **A systemic view.** This is the most distinguishing feature of lifelong learning. The lifelong learning framework views the demand for, and the supply of, learning opportunities as part of a connected system covering the whole lifecycle and comprising all forms of formal and informal learning.

- **The centrality of the learner.** This requires a shift in attention from a supply-side focus, for example on formal institutions and arrangements, to the demand side of meeting learner needs.

- **Motivation to learn.** This is an essential foundation for learning that continues throughout life. It requires attention to developing the capacity for "learning to learn" through self-paced and self-directed learning.

- **Multiple objectives of education.** The life-cycle view recognises the multiple goals of education – such as personal development, knowledge development, economic and social and cultural objectives – and that the priorities among these objectives may change over the life cycle.

📖 *Education Policy Analysis – 2001 Edition*, Chapter 1; "Lifelong Learning", *Policy Brief*, 2004.

Very high proportions of young adults – recently in the education system – have now completed upper secondary education ... An average of 78% of 25-34-year-olds in OECD countries now complete at least the upper secondary stage of education (2006). This stands as high as 90% or more in Canada, the Czech Republic, Finland, Korea, the Slovak Republic, and Sweden, as well as in the Russian Federation and Slovenia. The main watershed of participation in formal education used to be marked by completion of lower secondary schooling which in many countries corresponds to the end of compulsory education; this is clearly now shifting upwards to the next level.

... though not all enjoy such high attainment levels: Still only two-thirds or fewer of young adults in their mid-20s to mid-30s have reached the upper secondary level of attainment in Iceland (67%), Italy (67%), Poland (64%), Portugal (44%), and Spain (64%), and many fewer in Mexico (39%) and Turkey (37%). And even in those countries where completion is high, there is the "down-side" in the form of the relative disadvantage in which it places the minority of less than a quarter across OECD countries who now leave without finishing upper secondary education.

📖 *Education at a Glance: OECD Indicators – 2008 Edition*, Chapter A.

"Educational expectancy" – the number of years of study over a lifetime based on current participation patterns – is above 17 years on average: High "educational expectancy" reflects growing participation both before and after compulsory primary and secondary schooling. In 2004, in 24 of 28 OECD countries which supply data and 4 partner countries, people can expect to be in formal education for between 16 and 21 years. It is 19 years or more in Australia, Belgium, Denmark, Finland, Iceland, New Zealand, Sweden and the United Kingdom. It is less than 16 years in Luxembourg, Mexico, the Slovak Republic, Turkey, and the partner countries Chile, Israel, and the Russian Federation. "Expectancy" synthesises all current patterns and levels for different aged students into a single figure; it is not a prediction about how long a young child today might stay in education in the future.

📖 *Education at a Glance: OECD Indicators – 2006 Edition*, Chapter C.

Figure 6.1. **Expected time in education for 5-year-olds based on current enrolment patterns (2004)**

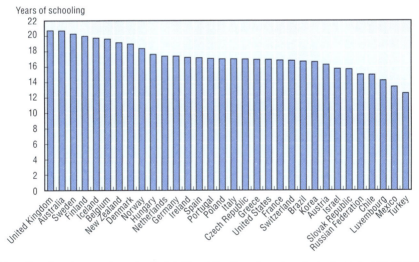

Note: The education expectancy is calculated by adding the net enrolment rates for each single year of age from age 5 onwards; the quantitative comparisons take no account of differing lengths of the school year, intensity of participation, or the quality of education across countries.

Source: OECD (2006), *Education at a Glance: OECD Indicators – 2006 Edition*, OECD Publishing, Paris.

StatLink 🔗 http://dx.doi.org/10.1787/555553154612

There are limits to the ever-lengthening duration of initial education, suggesting alternatives to universal long-cycle higher education are needed

to enhance skills and address inequity: OECD analysis of schooling and lifelong learning has identified social and cultural concerns about delaying the attainment of adulthood, and what this means for the healthy development of individuals and society as a whole. It needs to be asked how the interest of many young people in learning can be maintained if the expected duration of initial education is continually pushed outwards, affecting the goals of educational inclusion and the creation of the motivation to learn throughout life. The affordability of continually lengthening periods of initial education is also relevant to the sustainability of such developments.

📖 *Education Policy Analysis – 2004 Edition*, Chapter 3.

Progress towards the implementation of lifelong learning has been patchy, despite the sustained general expansion of initial education and training systems: A stock-taking of lifelong learning implementation for the 2001 OECD Education Ministers' meeting identified at that time four groups of countries. The Nordic countries stood out with good performance across multiple sectors. A second tier of countries – Canada, the Czech Republic, Germany, the Netherlands, and New Zealand – also did well albeit with certain gaps. A third tier, covering Australia, Switzerland, the United Kingdom, and the United States, was characterised by uneven performance on the available measures, especially of literacy. A fourth group – Ireland, Hungary, Portugal, and Poland – did poorly in comparison with other countries on most measures. A key issue is the importance of – but difficulty of implementing – a "whole of government" approach to lifelong learning.

📖 "Lifelong Learning", *Policy brief*, 2004; *Education Policy Analysis – 2001 Edition*, Chapter 2.

6.2. Orientations for policy

Lifelong learning is a crucial overarching aim of policy and development, including economic development, and calls for additional investment: A cogent statement on the importance of lifelong learning and the need for additional resources was made by German Minister Bulmahn to conclude the OECD policy conference on Co-financing Lifelong Learning. "Support for lifelong learning is essential for society as a whole. [It] is essential to ensure a smooth and equitable transition to a knowledge society, particularly in countries with ageing populations … Lifelong learning benefits individuals as well as businesses and society. Additional investments in lifelong learning are needed in view of the increasing share of services in the economy, the rapid technological change, an ageing society, the growing importance of knowledge and information in the value of production and extensive economic and social restructuring".

📖 *Co-financing Lifelong Learning: Towards a Systemic Approach*, 2004, Annex 1.

The lifelong learning framework offers directions for policy reform to address five systemic features:

- **Improving access, quality and equity:** Gaps in access are especially clear as regards very young children and older adults at either side of the main initial education system and these gaps need to be addressed. Access is not simply a matter of enrolment, however, and includes both the quality of the provision involved and the equity to ensure a fair and inclusive distribution of opportunities.

- **Ensuring foundation skills for all:** This requires not just universal access to basic education but improvements in young people's motivation to learn and their capacity for independent learning. Foundation skills are also needed by those adults who lack them.

- **Recognising all forms of learning, not just formal courses of study:** Learning takes many forms and occurs in many different settings, from formal courses in schools or colleges to various types of experience in families, communities and workplaces. All types of learning need to be recognised and made visible, according to their content, quality and outcomes rather than their location and form.

- **Mobilising resources, rethinking resource allocation across all sectors, settings and over the life-cycle:** Given that higher levels of participation increases costs, countries have used many different approaches to reduce them, especially teaching and personnel costs, rationalisation of the structure of provision, better use of ICTs, and more extensive use of the private sector.

- **Ensuring collaboration among a wide range of partners:** All lifelong learning involves stakeholders well beyond those covered by the educational authorities, and co-ordination in policy development and implementation is essential for success.

📖 "Lifelong Learning", *Policy brief*, 2004.

The overarching aim of lifelong learning applies as much to schools as it does to all other settings of education and training: There remains a tendency for school education to be assessed in its own terms rather than its broader success in laying the foundation for lifelong learning. Working towards lifelong learning in schools does not mean simply adding on whole new batteries of items to overloaded reform agendas. Rather, it demands developing the approaches which make learning central, including the motivation in individuals to continue to learn. It means adopting practices that encourage curiosity, innovation, creativity, and teamwork in students. It is about developing cultures of learning with appropriately diverse curricula and assessment methods, including assessment for learning. And schools must be staffed with teaching professionals suitably organised and equipped so they can do so.

📖 *Education Policy Analysis – 2004 Edition*, Chapter 3.

Make guidance more ambitious so that it aims to develop career-management skills, as well as providing information to certain groups for immediate decision-making: At present, services are largely available to limited numbers of groups, at fixed points in life, focused on immediate decisions. Lifelong learning and active labour market policies call for a wider and more fundamental role in developing career management in all learners and workers through services which are universally accessible throughout the lifespan – in ways, locations, and at times that reflect diverse client needs.

📖 *Career Guidance and Public Policy: Bridging the Gap*, 2004, Chapter 3.

Exploit the pivotal role of qualifications systems so as to promote dynamic lifelong education and training systems: Certain aspects of qualifications systems should receive attention in their implications for lifelong learning implementation, including:

- **Increase flexibility and responsiveness:** "Customisation" is one way to describe qualifications systems which are responsive to the changing needs of the economy, employment, and the personal ambitions of individuals. Flexibility is promoted by all the various mechanisms that increase choice.

- **Facilitate open access to qualifications:** An argument for lifelong learning is that individuals can gain qualifications from different starting points. Mechanisms to allow this include the development of new routes to existing qualifications, as will any effective information and guidance system that clarifies qualifications requirements.

- **Diversify assessment procedures:** Assessment methods (and the administration and cost associated with them) are an important influence on the willingness of individuals to engage in learning for a qualification. Credit transfer calls for different modes of assessment and outcomes-based methods also require greater diversity of assessment.

- **Make qualifications progressive:** Accumulating learning experiences and developing competences throughout life is now a central concept, and a significant shift from "once and for all" initial education and training. The key mechanisms here have to do with increasing coherence of the qualifications systems, such as through more developed qualifications frameworks or learning pathways.

📖 *Qualifications Systems: Bridges to Lifelong Learning*, 2007, Chapter 2.

ISBN 978-92-64-05989-4
Education Today
The OECD Perspective
© OECD 2009

Chapter 7

Outcomes, Benefits and Returns

Very rich information on educational outcomes has been generated through OECD work, especially with the triennial PISA achievement surveys. These survey the achievements of 15-year-olds in different competence areas, together with a growing range of associated background information, and in many non-member countries as well as those of the OECD. These surveys reveal the wide differences between countries. In charting patterns, very large numbers still do not attain at levels that might be regarded as the minimum for 21st century knowledge economies. The strong OECD focus on outcomes is set to expand beyond teenage achievements as surveys of adult competences and outcomes from higher education are in development. There is also expanding analysis of returns to education within OECD, including outside the Directorate for Education. Findings confirm the positive returns to higher levels of educational attainment on a variety of measures, certainly for the individual, though with much more to be done to make educational benefits more transparent to learners themselves.

7.1. Key findings and conclusions

Among OECD countries, students in Finland and Korea, with non-members Chinese Taipei and Hong Kong-China, perform above the other countries in mathematics: In these countries in 2006 the mean scores in mathematics were closely grouped between 549 and 547, some way above the next-highest scoring country, the Netherlands (531). Compared with an OECD average of 13.4% attaining the top levels 5 and 6, 27.1% do so in Korea and even more do at 31.9% and 27.7% in Chinese Taipei and Hong Kong-China, respectively. At least one in five students are proficient in complex mathematics tasks, at PISA level 5 or 6, in Finland, Switzerland, Belgium and the Netherlands. In these countries, significant pools exist of young people with high-level mathematical skills who are likely to play a crucial role in advancing the knowledge economy.
📖 *PISA 2006 – Volume 1: Analysis*, 2007, Chapter 6.

Very few countries do not escape having significant minorities, or even a majority, of students with very low performance in mathematics: With the exception of Finland and Korea, all OECD countries have at least 10% of students who achieve at only PISA level 1 or below. In 13 OECD countries (Austria, France, Greece, Hungary, Italy, Luxembourg, Mexico, Norway, Portugal, the Slovak Republic, Spain, Turkey, the United States) this accounts for a fifth or more of the students. The lowest-achieving students in mathematics are actually the majority of 15-year-olds in Mexico (56.5%).
📖 *PISA 2006 – Volume 1: Analysis*, 2007, Chapter 6.

Low spread in student performance can go hand-in-hand with high levels of excellence: Six of the countries with the smallest differences in the range defined by the mathematics score which marks the cut-off between the top quarter of students and the rest (75th percentile) and between the three-quarters mark and below (25th percentile) – Canada, Finland, Iceland, Ireland, Japan and Korea – all perform significantly above the OECD average in 2000. Four of these with low spread in maths scores – Canada, Finland, Japan and Korea – are among the six best-performing OECD countries in mathematics literacy (the others in the top six being Australia and New Zealand). Hence, significant numbers achieving at a high level does not automatically bring with it widening gaps with the others.
📖 *Education at a Glance: OECD Indicators – 2004 Edition*, Chapter A.

In only 5 OECD countries do more than two-thirds of young people reach or surpass PISA level 3 in reading literacy – the level which involves comprehension and interpretation of moderately complex text: The five countries are Canada, Finland, Ireland, Korea, and New Zealand. The average attaining level 3 or above across all OECD countries is 57.1%. Having a high proportion achieving this basic threshold level does not automatically mean that the country has among the highest numbers of top performers: the proportion in Korea attaining the top level 5 (21.7%) is nearly double that achieved in Ireland (11.7%).

📖 PISA 2006 – Volume 1: Analysis, 2007, Chapter 6.

In 18 OECD countries, 40% or more do not achieve at the level 3 threshold in reading literacy, and these low-performing students are in the majority in four of these countries: The countries which have 40% or more achieving at best at levels 2 are Austria, the Czech Republic, Denmark, France, Germany, Japan, Greece, Hungary, Iceland, Italy, Luxembourg, Mexico, Norway, Portugal, the Slovak Republic, Spain, Turkey, and the United Kingdom. They are the majority of students in Greece, Italy, Mexico, Portugal, the Slovak Republic, Spain, and Turkey.

📖 PISA 2006 – Volume 1: Analysis, 2007, Chapter 6.

Figure 7.1. **Percentages in each PISA proficiency level in science (2006)**

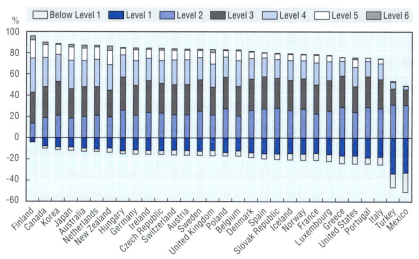

Note: Countries are ordered left to right in descending percentages of 15-year-olds at levels 2 and over.
Source: OECD (2007), PISA 2006 – Volume 1: Analysis, OECD Publishing, Paris.

StatLink 📊 http://dx.doi.org/10.1787/141844475532

Figure 7.2. **Percentages in each PISA proficiency level in mathematics (2006)**

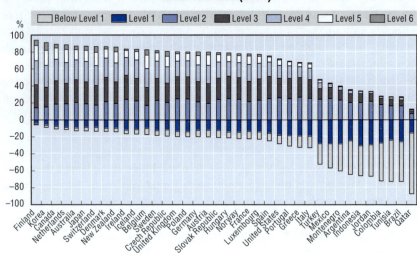

Note: Countries are ordered left to right in descending percentages of 15-year-olds at levels 2 and over.
Source: OECD (2007), PISA 2006 – Volume 1: Analysis, OECD Publishing, Paris.

StatLink ᵐᔆᴾ http://dx.doi.org/10.1787/142046885031

Figure 7.3. **Percentages in each PISA proficiency level in reading (2006)**

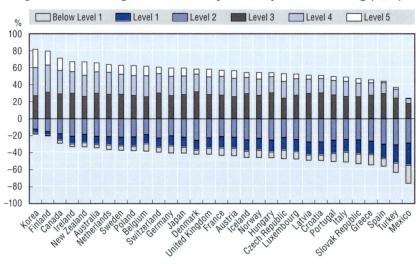

Note: Countries are ordered left to right in descending percentages of 15-year-olds at levels 2 and over.
Source: OECD (2007), PISA 2006 – Volume 1: Analysis, OECD Publishing, Paris.

StatLink ᵐᔆᴾ http://dx.doi.org/10.1787/142046885031

EDUCATION TODAY: THE OECD PERSPECTIVE – ISBN 978-92-64-05989-4 – © OECD 2009

The top performers in science among OECD countries are Finland, followed by Australia, Canada, Japan, Korea, the Netherlands and New Zealand: With OECD countries fixed at an average of 500, the top performer on the combined science scale in 2006 was Finland clearly ahead at 563. Australia, Canada, Japan, Korea, the Netherlands, and New Zealand are the next group of top-performing OECD countries in science, all at 522 or above. On average in these countries, only 1.3% of 15-year-olds reach the top level 6 but in Finland and New Zealand over 3.9% do so. The percentage of these very top science performers is also relatively high (between 2.1 and 2.9%) in Australia, Canada, Japan, and the United Kingdom.

📖 *PISA 2006 – Volume 1: Analysis*, 2007, Chapter 2.

The gender gap in science performance is small: For most OECD countries there are no statistically significant differences in science performance between young women and men. In 6 of these countries – Denmark, Luxembourg, Mexico, the Netherlands, Switzerland, and the United Kingdom – there is a male advantage but it is relatively small (between 6 and 10 points). In Turkey and Greece, a somewhat larger female advantage in science (11-12 points) was found in 2006.

📖 *PISA 2006 – Volume 1: Analysis*, 2007, Chapter 2.

Investment in early childhood education and care brings significant returns to individuals and society: Research from diverse countries suggests a common conclusion that the investment in young children brings significant benefits not only for children and families, but also for society at large. High quality early childhood services lay a strong foundation of learning which is fundamental to the rest of the lives of the individuals involved. Children from disadvantaged background in particular benefit from acquiring such a foundation. Early childhood investments bring significant educational, social, economic and labour market returns; improved transitions from one educational level to the next and higher achievement; and lower crime rates among teenagers. Lack of investment in children's services can result in child-care shortages and unequal access, even segregation, of children according to income. Unavailability of services raises barriers against women's full-time employment – with the economic and social consequences which flow from that – and tends to channel women towards low-paid, part-time jobs.

📖 *Starting Strong II: Early Childhood Education and Care*, 2006, Annex D.

Attaining at least upper secondary education is an important hedge against the risk of unemployment: The unemployment rate among those adults aged 25-64 years with an upper secondary education is clearly lower than among those who have not gone further than the lower secondary level – on average 4.2 percentage points lower in 2006. This gap is particularly high in the eastern European OECD countries of the Czech Republic (16.8 percentage gap) and the Slovak Republic (34), and in Germany (10), and in these three the gap has grown markedly over the past decade. Expressing this upper secondary advantage as a ratio of unemployment rates, those with upper secondary education are half or less than half as likely to be unemployed compared with those with lower secondary education in Austria, the Czech Republic, Denmark, Germany, Hungary, Norway, the Slovak Republic, and Switzerland. There is a small number of countries – Greece, Korea, Mexico, and Turkey – where there is no greater unemployment risk among those finishing education at the lower, compared with the upper, secondary level.

📖 *Education at a Glance: OECD Indicators – 2008 Edition*, Chapter A.

In some countries the earnings pay-off of acquiring an upper secondary education is considerable ... The countries with the highest earnings advantage of those with upper secondary compared with lower secondary education for all working-age adults are Austria, Korea, Portugal, Turkey, the United Kingdom, and the United States; in these countries, those with the lower attainments earn around only two-thirds to 70% of upper secondary graduates. The gaps for these particular countries tend to narrow somewhat for younger as compared with all adults, especially in Korea where the gap disappears, though in Austria and Turkey in particular the income difference stays much the same whether for younger or all adults. Turkish women of all ages and especially in the younger age bracket earn less than half the incomes of Turkish women with upper secondary education.

... but not everywhere does completing upper secondary education represent an important earnings threshold: There are countries in which the earnings advantage of upper secondary over those who left education with no more than lower secondary attainments is not particularly marked – the lower attainers earn 90% or more of those with upper secondary education. In these cases instead, the main difference is between those who finished with secondary-level compared with tertiary-level attainment. Of the 25 countries supplying the data to permit such calculations for adults aged 25 to 64 years these are Belgium (for men), Finland, and Germany (men); among younger adults aged 25-34, this narrower advantage is found in Australia (men), Belgium (men), Finland, Germany (men), Korea (women, where younger women with lower secondary attainment earn 1.26 *more* than those with upper secondary education), the Netherlands (men), and Spain (men).

📖 *Education at a Glance: OECD Indicators – 2008 Edition*, Chapter A.

Figure 7.4. **Earnings from employment by level of educational attainment for 25-to-64-years-olds by gender, 2006 or latest available year**

Upper secondary and post-secondary non-tertiary education = 100

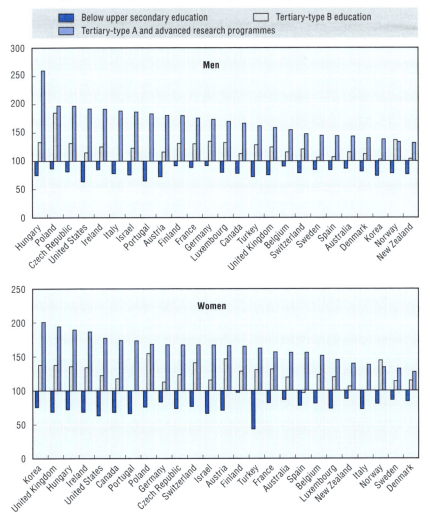

Source: OECD (2008), *Education at a Glance: OECD Indicators – 2008 Edition*, OECD Publishing, Paris.

StatLink http://dx.doi.org/10.1787/401781614508

There is a strong positive relationship between education and the average earnings of individuals, with marked premiums for those with tertiary-level attainments: In all countries, graduates of tertiary education earn substantially more than upper secondary graduates who in turn earn more than those whose attainment does not go beyond basic education. The earnings premium of tertiary graduates has gone up in most countries over the past 10 years, especially in Germany, Hungary, Ireland, and Italy (but with some exceptions – New Zealand and Spain). Earnings differentials between higher education and upper secondary graduates are generally greater than between upper and lower secondary graduates. The earnings premium for tertiary over upper secondary graduates, all adult ages and men and women combined, ranges from a high of 2.19 times the incomes of the upper secondary group in Hungary to a low of 1.15 higher in New Zealand.

📖 *Education at a Glance: OECD Indicators – 2008 Edition*, Chapter A.

Factoring in the costs of acquiring the next higher level of education to arrive at "private rates of return" shows that, on average, it always pays to continue to upper over lower secondary education ... For men and women, continuing on to upper secondary education after the lower secondary level pays off on average in all countries. For men, this "private" rate of return stands at 10% or more in 8 of the 19 countries, with the range lying between 6.1% (France) and 6.7% (Denmark) to 18% (the United Kingdom) and 17.5% (the United States). The range is greater for women, lying between 1.5% in Korea and four countries (Denmark, France, Norway and Switzerland) where it stands between 5% and 6%, up to 15.6% (United States) and 18.5% (United Kingdom).

... with even higher average pay-offs for continuing on to tertiary over upper secondary education: The relative advantage of continuing on to acquire tertiary over upper secondary education is also positive in all the countries with data, with even larger incentives to continue. For men, it is 10% or more in 10 of the 19 countries (lowest in Denmark [4.4%] and Sweden [5.1%]) and in the same number of countries for women (again with Denmark and Sweden with the lowest returns). The rate of return advantage of continuing to tertiary beyond upper secondary rises to 20% or more for men in the Czech Republic, Hungary (19.8%), Poland and Portugal, and for women in the Czech Republic and Portugal.

📖 *Education at a Glance: OECD Indicators – 2008 Edition*, Chapter A.

International comparisons show that education plays a pivotal role in fostering labour productivity and economic growth: A country able to attain literacy scores 1% higher than the international average will achieve levels of labour productivity and GDP per capita that are 2.5 and 1.5% higher respectively than those of other countries. Literacy scores as measures of human capital have higher associations with economic growth than indicators of schooling. The International Adult Literacy Survey offers two explanations as to why this might be so: literacy might be a superior measure of some key driver of growth and data on literacy might be more comparable than that on educational attainment.

📖 *Education at a Glance: OECD Indicators – 2006 Edition*, Chapter A; Coulombe *et al.*, 2004.

Low adult literacy and competency scores are strongly associated with the risks of unemployment and insecurity: The first Adult Literacy and Life Skills Survey measured adults' prose, document, numeracy and problem-solving skills across five broad levels of proficiency. Level 3 is identified as the suitable minimum for managing the demands of work and daily life. Based on data gathered from Canada, Italy, Norway, Switzerland, the United States, and the Mexican State of Nuevo Leon, as well as Bermuda:

- Individuals whose numeracy scores are at levels 1 and 2 are two to three times more likely to be outside the labour force for six or more months than those with higher scores.
- For young adults, proficiency in document literacy and numeracy is strongly associated with finding employment; young adults scoring at levels 1 and 2 are more likely to stay unemployed for longer periods of time.

📖 *Learning a Living: First Results of the Adult Literacy and Life Skills Survey*, 2005.

More years of schooling are associated with better health and well-being, enhancing the social returns to educational investment via lower health expenditure: There are *direct* effects of education on health via changes in individual behaviour; *indirect* effects of education on health, such as those via income; and *intergenerational* effects of educated parents on the health of their children. Important though hard to quantify are the benefits which come with the enhancement of well-being and the quality of life: as well as preventing illness or enabling its more efficient treatment, education enables people to live more positively healthy lives. The "cost containment" benefits are more open to measurement, and simulation studies have proposed estimates for the health savings that might flow from raising attainment by an additional year of education or ensuring that all attain basic qualifications.

📖 *Understanding the Social Outcomes of Learning*, 2007, Chapter 5.

Training enhances wages and job prospects, especially for younger, mobile and highly-educated workers: Adult education and training have a significant impact on both worker productivity and wage levels. Diverse national and international panel studies (altogether covering 13 European countries and the United States) have come up with wage premiums resulting from participation in training courses ranging from negligible in France to 2.5% annually in Germany and 5% in Portugal. Training tends also to reduce the chance of being unemployed and increases chances of reemployment in the case of lay-off. The wage gains associated with the training are improved when workers move on from their employers; the higher premiums come from learning taken with previous employers and with the best results for young and highly-educated workers.

📖 *Promoting Adult Learning*, 2005, Chapter 2; Ok and Tergeist, 2003; *Employment Outlook – 2004 Edition*, Chapter 4.

7.2. Orientations for policy

Improve educational outcomes for all through more challenging and supportive learning environments as a way of maintaining economic competitiveness: OECD countries' capacity to compete in the global knowledge economy depends on whether they can meet the fast-growing demand for high-level skills. This in turn will hinge on significant improvements in the quality of schooling outcomes and a more equitable distribution of learning opportunities. Education systems need to develop more challenging and more supportive learning environments and be more effective and flexible in improving learning outcomes.

📖 *Education at a Glance: OECD Indicators – 2006 Edition*, Editorial.

Foster student interest in science, mathematics and technology education as an explicit objective: Recognising that a declining interest in studying science, mathematics and technology is of particular concern in many countries, and considering that students' motivation and engagement in these areas closely relate to their achievement and potentially to their future career choices, the OECD encourages educational policies and practices that foster students' interest and engagement in science, mathematics and technology. The OECD also suggests to place greater emphasis on engaging female students in these subject areas.

📖 *Education Policy Analysis – 2006 Edition*, Chapter 5.

Countries should aim to secure similar student performance among schools: Low "between-school variation" means that there is no obvious advantage in terms of performance for a student to attend one school as opposed to another – they all perform to broadly equal levels. In three countries – Norway, Finland and Iceland – less than 10% of variation in mathematics achievement in 2003 was accounted for by such differences; all the rest of the variation is "within-school". The OECD average is much higher than 10% and stands at almost exactly a third. The countries where it is over 60% are Turkey, Hungary and Japan. Securing similar student performance among schools is both important in itself as a policy goal and is compatible with high overall performance standards.

📖 *Education at a Glance: OECD Indicators – 2006 Edition*, Chapter A.

A broad framework of fundamental competences can inform assessment: Education and lifelong learning systems can be assessed in terms of their success in developing the key competences needed to function in today's complex demanding society, which go well beyond any particular level or educational setting. Three clusters of such key competences have been elaborated through the OECD DeSeCo Project ("The Definition and Selection of Key Competences", 2004), each further divided into three components:

1. **Using tools interactively:** a) The ability to use language, symbols and text interactively; b) The ability to use knowledge and information interactively; c) The ability to use technology interactively.

2. **Interacting in heterogeneous groups:** a) The ability to relate well to others; b) The ability to co-operate; c) The ability to manage and resolve conflicts.

3. **Acting autonomously:** a) The ability to act within the big picture; b) The ability to form and conduct life plans and personal projects; c) The ability to assert rights, interests, limits and needs.

Invest in analyses to reveal the returns and make more precise the benefits of different patterns of lifelong learning: The vitality of the public debate on lifelong learning has depended heavily on the assumption that it is a sound investment – for economies, societies and individuals. To date, the evidence is very thin. Preliminary work by the OECD provides encouraging results but such work needs to be broadened to more countries and fine-tuned. It needs to consider not only average returns to learning over the lifetime but the dispersion of returns in order to clarify the extent and distribution of the risks entailed by the investment.

📖 *Co-financing Lifelong Learning: Towards a Systemic Approach*, 2004, Chapter 4.

Clarify and improve returns to training by augmenting available information and removing structural barriers ... Efforts to improve research and dissemination of information can help convince individuals and firms of the benefits involved. Cost/benefit analysis provides information that can encourage and motivate adults to engage in learning as well as clarifying who should cover the financial costs. Evidence of other social and personal effects such as useful course content, greater self-esteem and increased social interaction can also help improve participation. Efforts to stimulate firms to invest in training can be assisted by promoting the transparency of human capital investments in company accounting. Acting directly on increasing the returns to training through alternative mechanisms, such as embedding skill improvements in the wage determination process, can improve training take-up and firm productivity.

... and by making the outcomes transparent – and easily signalled to individuals and firms: The development of national qualifications systems provides a sort of currency in this respect. Recognition of informal and non-formal learning can contribute to reducing the opportunity cost of learning. Experience shows that many countries are adopting the practice because the benefits can be substantial and can help realise a culture of lifelong learning. 📖 *Promoting Adult Learning*, 2005, Chapter 2.

ISBN 978-92-64-05989-4
Education Today
The OECD Perspective
© OECD 2009

Chapter 8

Equity and Equality of Opportunity

Analyses of developments and policies that influence equity have been an underlying priority in much of the OECD educational work. The persistent patterns of inequality have been highlighted, with the increasingly quality of international data permitting analyses relating to many pertinent groups of learners and their educational experiences. OECD analysis has shown that there need be no contradiction between equity and efficiency, and indeed has underlined how damaging to economic as well as social goals is the phenomenon of exclusion and widespread under-achievement. A major international review of equity in education, published in 2007, outlines ten broad policy directions around the design of provision, practices, and resourcing. The charting of the opportunities, outcomes and policies towards different population groups who may well be disadvantaged has been undertaken across the many sectors of education and training, including longstanding work on special educational needs.

8.1. Key findings and conclusions

There is no contradiction between equity and efficiency in education:
There is a widespread argument that the redistribution of resources to those
in greatest need helps equity but damages efficiency. The OECD in its analysis of
equity, as well as the World Bank in a recent report, argue that equity and
efficiency are in fact complementary. This is clearly the case within basic
education: school failure has large costs not only to those involved, but also to
society, because the welfare costs of marginalised persons are large. Reasonably-
priced, effective measures to address failure benefit both efficiency and equity.
Some analyses even suggest that an equitable distribution of skills across
populations has a strong impact on overall economic performance.

📖 *No More Failures: Ten Steps to Equity in Education*, 2007, Chapter 1; World
Bank, 2005.

**The countries with high quality and high equity have embraced
student heterogeneity and avoided premature and differentiated structures:**
Evidence from PISA (and comparison with evidence at the primary school
phase from the Progress in International Reading Literacy Study [PIRLS]) and
from countries which have introduced comprehensive schooling, suggests that
early tracking is associated with reduced equity in outcomes and sometimes
weakens results overall. In countries with early selection of students into highly
differentiated education systems, differences among schools are large and
the relationship between socio-economic background and student school
performance stronger.

📖 *No More Failures: Ten Steps to Equity in Education*, 2007, Chapter 3.

**The general upgrading of attainments and qualifications increasingly
excludes those who have not shared in this advance:** Many adults remain
unqualified and some young people still do not successfully complete secondary
education. Across the OECD nearly one in three adults (31%) has only primary or
lower secondary education – a real disadvantage in terms of employment and life
chances. In all OECD countries, those with weak basic qualifications are much
less likely to continue learning in adult life and there are big differences between
countries. That there are fewer proportionately with these very low attainment
and qualification levels increases the risk of their exclusion and detachment
from economic and social life.

📖 *No More Failures: Ten Steps to Equity in Education*, 2007, Chapter 2.

Choice may stimulate quality but with risks for equity: There are quality arguments to be made in favour of creating a degree of choice as a vehicle for stimulating improvement. When choices exist, schools must then look beyond their own walls at what others – their potential "competitors" – are doing; without some room for "exit" to be exercised, parents and students have no threat to back up "voice" or participation. OECD work confirms that better educated, middle-class parents are more likely to avail themselves of choice opportunities and send their children to what they perceive to be the best school, widening the gaps between the sought-after schools and the rest. Across countries, greater choice in school systems is associated with larger differences in the social composition of different schools.

📖 *No More Failures: Ten Steps to Equity in Education*, 2007, Chapter 3; *Demand-sensitive Schooling? Evidence and Issues*, 2006.

Girls and women have now moved clearly ahead of boys and men in education: The number of expected years in education between ages 15 and 29 years across OECD countries enjoyed by young women – 7 years – now surpasses those of young men who average only 6.6. It was higher in all countries in 2006 except Australia, Austria, Germany, Japan, Mexico, the Netherlands, Switzerland and (in 2005) Turkey among OECD countries. Female graduation rates from upper secondary education are higher in 22 of the 24 countries permitting the comparison – the exceptions being Switzerland and Turkey. The female advantage gap is more than 10 percentage points in Denmark, Iceland, Ireland, New Zealand, Norway, and Spain. Only in Japan, Korea, Switzerland and Turkey do the entry rates of men to tertiary education now exceed those of women.

📖 *Education at a Glance: OECD Indicators – 2008 Edition*, Chapters A and C.

Relatively small proportions of compulsory school students receive additional funding for their education due to special needs, though there are cases where this amounts to 1 in 5 students: In the countries supplying data on additional funding across the three categories of needs (disabilities, difficulties and disadvantages), a nearly 3% median of students (2.7%) receive additional outlays because they are assessed as disabled, rising to just over 5% in the United States. Additional spending on those with difficulties is in general low (2.4%) rising to 3.3% for those counted as "disadvantaged". Much higher proportions are found in some countries – such as the 17% of United Kingdom compulsory students qualifying for funding due to learning difficulties, or the 15% and over in the Netherlands, Flemish Belgium, the United States, and Mexico because of their disadvantage.

📖 *Students with Disabilities, Learning Difficulties and Disadvantages: Policies, Statistics and Indicators – 2007 Edition*, Chapter 4.

Figure 8.1. **Women have overtaken men in upper secondary and higher education attainments, as shown by attainments of different age groups in the adult population in 2006**

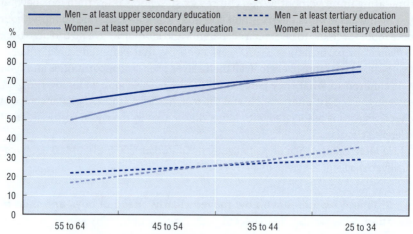

Source: OECD (2008), Education at a Glance: OECD Indicators – 2008 Edition, OECD Publishing, Paris.

StatLink http://dx.doi.org/10.1787/401474646362

Figure 8.2. **Mathematics performance by migration status in 2003**

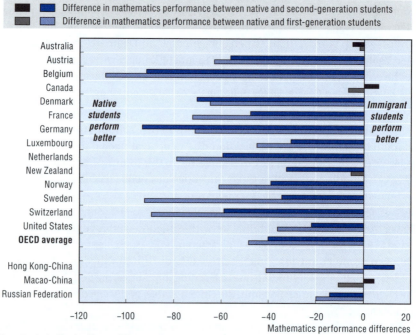

Note: Statistically significant differences are marked in blue tones.

Source: OECD (2007), Education at a Glance: OECD Indicators – 2007 Edition, OECD Publishing, Paris.

StatLink http://dx.doi.org/10.1787/068061288083

Boys with disabilities and receiving additional resources outnumber such girls by approximately 60 to 40, rising to two-thirds to one-third in their call on specific resources for learning and behavioural difficulties: These are consistent results, repeatedly found in different studies with different methodologies. There is a consistent majority of males over females in special needs education provision or in receipt of additional resources for disabilities and learning difficulties. Whether done by location (special school, special class, regular class), cross-nationally or nationally, age of student or stage of education, boys outnumber girls. For learning difficulties, the difference is even larger with males outnumbering females by two-thirds to one-third.

📖 *Students with Disabilities, Learning Difficulties and Disadvantages: Policies, Statistics and Indicators – 2007 Edition*, Chapter 4.

Immigrant students tend to perform at levels significantly lower than their native peers, though with some notable exceptions: The degree to which immigrants lag behind native students is most pronounced in Austria, Belgium, Denmark, France, Germany, the Netherlands, and Switzerland, though in some places they are at similar levels – in three traditional settlement countries Australia, Canada, and New Zealand, as well as in Macao-China. Second-generation students perform significantly better than first-generation in Canada, Luxembourg, Sweden, Switzerland, and Hong Kong-China. There is lower performance despite generally positive attitudes towards learning among immigrant students and there is not a significant association between the size of the immigrant student populations and the performance difference between immigrant and native students.

📖 *Where Immigrant Students Succeed: A Comparative Review of Performance and Engagement in PISA 2003*, 2006, Chapter 2.

In many OECD countries, tertiary education remains dominated by students from well-educated backgrounds: Evidence from the 1990s showed that young people whose parents had tertiary education themselves were between two to six times as likely to complete tertiary studies as those whose parents had only secondary level qualifications. Only a few countries have data to permit such calculations; among those that do, students with fathers who had completed higher education were more than twice as likely to be in higher education in Austria, France, Germany, Portugal and the United Kingdom. It is substantially less in Spain (1.5 as likely) and Ireland (1.1). Countries providing more equal access to higher education – such as Finland, Ireland and Spain – are also the countries with the more equal between-school performances in PISA 2000.

📖 *No More Failures: Ten Steps to Equity in Education*, 2007; *Education at a Glance: OECD Indicators – 2007 Edition*, Chapter A.

Social background strongly influences teenage expectations to go on to complete higher education, with the influence seen most powerfully in the Slovak Republic, Switzerland, and Hungary: PISA information on students' social backgrounds allows their categorisation into "high" and "low" socio-economic status and the comparison between them regarding their expectations to complete higher education. In all countries, there is a clear relationship between expectations to get an advanced education and social background, with the odds mainly in the range 2.0 to 2.9. The odds are lowest – expectations least shaped by background – in Finland (1.8). They are over 2.9 in Austria (3.0), Belgium (3.0), Greece (3.0), the Slovak Republic (3.1), and Switzerland (3.1), rising to 4.0 in Hungary.

📖 *Education at a Glance: OECD Indicators – 2007 Edition*, Chapter A.

Countries share the fact of large inequalities in access to adult learning: The disadvantaged groups regarding adult learning are mainly the low-educated, older individuals and those working in small- and medium-sized enterprises. There are no common trends relating to employment status. While the employed have higher participation rates in half the countries supplying evidence, the unemployed have higher participation in four, and those out of the labour force in another four.

📖 *Promoting Adult Learning*, 2005, Chapter 1.

8.2. Orientations for policy

The OECD advances ten steps – major policy recommendations which would reduce school failure and dropout, make society fairer and avoid the large social costs of marginalised adults with few basic skills. These concern **design** (points 1-4), **practices** (5-7), and **resourcing** (8-10):

1. **Limit early tracking and streaming and postpone academic selection:** The OECD suggests careful review of early differentiation into schools of different types in those education systems that practise it and holds strong reservations about introducing it in those education systems that do not. The early tracking and streaming of school students need to be justified in terms of proven benefits given that it so often poses a risk to equity. Systems that use early tracking should consider raising the age when it first takes place and academic selection needs to be used with caution.

2. **Manage school choice so as to contain the risks to equity:** The exercise of choice poses risks to equity and requires careful management to ensure that it does not increase the differences in social composition of different schools. When there is the exercise of parental choice, the oversubscribed schools need to find ways to even out the social mix – such as through lottery systems as selection methods – and financial premiums to schools with disadvantaged students may also help.

3. **In upper secondary education, provide attractive alternatives, remove dead ends and prevent dropout:** Early prevention of dropout is the best cure and monitoring those at risk should be linked to interventions to improve outcomes and prevent dropout. Basic schooling should support those who are struggling rather than focus primarily on those who excel. Upper secondary education should be attractive, offering good quality pathways with effective links to the world of work. Special programmes to smooth the transitions at the end of basic schooling can help encourage students to stay in school. Good quality vocational tracks are essential: removing an academic hurdle from entrance to general upper secondary education, as Norway and Sweden have done, can serve to increase the status of vocational tracks.

4. **Offer second chances to gain from education:** Second chances are necessary for those who lack basic education and skills. These include programmes that provide literacy training, primary and secondary education, work-based programmes and arrangements to recognise informal learning. Across OECD countries, many adults and young dropouts without basic education obtain school qualifications through second chance programmes. In the United States, almost 60% of dropouts eventually earn a high school credential (GED certificate).

5. **Provide systematic help to those who fall behind in school and reduce high rates of school-year repetition:** The high repetition rates in some countries should be reduced. They should change incentives to schools so that they do not so readily use repetition and instead develop alternatives for those who are struggling. One way is through greater interventions in classrooms which have proved to be effective in addressing learning needs of weaker students, like the Finnish approach of offering a sequence of intensifying interventions for those with difficulties to draw them back into the mainstream. Teachers need a highly-developed professional repertoire aimed at supporting those who are falling behind.

6. **Strengthen the links between school and home especially for disadvantaged families:** Parental involvement – working with children at home and actively participating in school activities – improves results. Disadvantaged parents tend to be among the least involved: schools need to target their efforts to improve communication with the most disadvantaged parents and help develop environments conducive to learning in homes. After-school homework clubs offer one way to support those with weak home support.

7. **Respond to diversity and provide for the successful inclusion of migrants and minorities within mainstream education:** Incentives to encourage immigrants into early childhood education are important. Particular attention needs to be given to language learning at all levels, including through teacher professional development – for this and for all other aspects of teaching in

multicultural environments. At the same time, segregation must be avoided including the tendency for too many immigrant children to end up in special education institutions.

8. **Provide strong education for all, giving priority to early childhood provision and basic schooling:** Where fees are involved in early childhood education, they should be moderate and remitted for those too poor to pay. Countries which charge fees for early childhood but not tertiary education need to re-examine their policies on equity grounds. A strong focus is needed in basic education on those with learning difficulties, and the implicit incentive for some to drop out provided by linking grants to families with school performance means that this practice should be reviewed on equity grounds.

9. **Direct resources to the students with the greatest needs, so that poorer communities enjoy at least the same level of provision as others better-off, and to support schools in difficulty:** Countries need adequate mechanisms to redistribute resources and minimise regional inequities in provision with the aim of reaching acceptable minimum standards everywhere. Additional resources need to be channelled through schools to help disadvantaged students while the stigma of labelling particular schools as "for disadvantaged students" should be avoided.

10. **Set concrete targets for more equity, particularly related to low school attainment and dropouts:** Numerical targets are a useful policy lever through articulating clearly what is to be achieved rather than simply the means to improvement. Countries can usefully adopt a small number of numerical targets, particularly for reducing the numbers of school-leavers with poor basic skills and of early school dropouts. Policy needs also to manage and respond to the public debate which follows publication of school-level test results, so that it does not exacerbate the equity problems themselves, and it should give energetic support to those schools with weak results.

📖 *No More Failures: Ten Steps to Equity in Education*, 2007, Summary and Policy Recommendations.

Equity for students with special needs requires sustainable inclusive education policies, with a resource-based approach to satisfy individuals' needs: A resource-based approach to special needs helps to quantify how needs are being met, but the additional resources should be used efficiently and effectively in enhancing inclusion in school settings and access to the labour market. Equity in access for students with disabilities, difficulties and disadvantages depends on effective co-ordination between welfare, health and education services and with the private and independent sectors. Inclusive education requires all those who work in educational settings to have some understanding of special needs issues and of the ways in which other non-teaching professionals work. Sustainability of inclusion policies is

EDUCATION TODAY: THE OECD PERSPECTIVE – ISBN 978-92-64-05989-4 – © OECD 2009

limited because the training of teachers, academics and other professionals to work in such situations is under-developed.

📖 *Students with Disabilities, Learning Difficulties and Disadvantages: Statistics and Indicators*, 2005.

Policy actions to improve the situation of the Young Adults with Low Levels of Education (YALLE) group need more precise targeting criteria than age or qualification level: The YALLE group is heterogeneous. The disadvantages often experienced by immigrant populations call for specific programmes, with young women facing particular challenges in connection with their family conditions and specific national family or employment policies. Programmes for re-qualification should be sensitive to specific structures of national labour markets, including at the local level, and the demand for different occupations and qualifications.

📖 *From Education to Work: A Difficult Transition for Young Adults with Low Levels of Education*, 2005, Chapter 6.

Understanding effective approaches for teaching, assessment and learning are just as much a priority for adults needing language, literacy and numeracy skills (LLN) as for school and tertiary students: The LLN sector has traditionally been set apart from the mainstream and consequently been relatively neglected. Among the priorities for addressing the learning needs of adults with low foundation skills are:

- **Strengthen professionalism:** Countries need to continue in the current direction of strengthening practice through more rigorous qualification and professional development requirements.

- **Balance structure and flexibility:** Formative assessment is a very helpful organising framework to do this.

- **Strengthen learner-centred approaches:** Many aspects of adult LLN provision are still more oriented to the needs of systems rather than learners.

- **Diversify approaches to assessment and programme evaluation for accountability:** Systems which use diverse, well-aligned measures of learning processes as well as outcomes will be better able to manage competing goals and interests – and to capture useful data.

- **Strengthen the knowledge base:** Researchers in the field will need to broaden the range of methodologies used and in particular to pay much greater attention to impact.

📖 *Teaching, L.earning and Assessment for Adults: Improving Foundation Skills*, 2008, Chapter 11.

ISBN 978-92-64-05989-4
Education Today
The OECD Perspective
© OECD 2009

Chapter 9

Innovation and Knowledge Management

Recognition of the key role of research and knowledge management in educational practice and policy-making is in general recent. In many countries, there has been only weak capacity to develop and exploit the knowledge base on which improved practice and effective policies can be based. The volume of relevant educational R&D tends generally to be low, despite education being so explicitly about knowledge. Similarly, a great deal of educational change is still shaped by short-term considerations despite education's fundamental long-term mission and nature. Educational R&D systems, knowledge management, futures thinking, and evidence-informed policy and practice, have all been prominent aspects of the OECD work done primarily through the Centre for Educational Research and Innovation.

9.1. Key findings and conclusions

The growing focus on educational outcomes has resulted in both an explosion of evidence of different kinds and a policy thirst for the results of educational research: There is a mounting preoccupation with what happens *as a result of* educational investments and participation, rather than the primary focus being on these inputs. Outcomes cover not only course completion and qualifications, but also skills and competences (as with the PISA surveys), access to and success in the labour market, and wider social outcomes such as health and citizenship attributable to education. There has been a huge expansion of evidence resulting from the growing volume of testing and assessment activities. As policy increasingly focuses on what education actually delivers, so is there interest in the information coming from research, but we know too little about how this evidence is used and whether it is used effectively.

📖 *Evidence in Education: Linking Research and Policy*, 2007, Chapter 1.

Educational R&D is not given the support it needs to effect change and promote innovation: Despite the key role of knowledge-based innovation in education, the country reviews of educational R&D have confirmed the following features as commonly (though not universally) characterising OECD systems:

- Low levels of investment in educational research.
- Generally low levels of research capacity, especially in quantitative research.
- Weak links between research, policy and innovation.

📖 *New Challenges for Educational Research*, 2003, Chapter 1.

Schools are conventionally poor at using the key motors of innovation – research knowledge, networking, modular restructuring, technological advance: OECD work on knowledge management has identified four key "pumps of innovation":

- The "science-based" innovation pump: education has not traditionally made enough direct use of research knowledge, and there is often cultural resistance to doing so. This is increasingly being targeted in reform.
- The "horizontally-organised" innovation pump: there are obvious benefits in terms of teachers pooling their knowledge through networks, but incentives to do so remain underdeveloped. There is need to tighten the "loose coupling"

between the single teachers, individual classrooms, and individual schools that so characterises school systems.

- The "modular structures" pump: this is about building complex processes from smaller subsystems that are designed independently but function together. Education is accustomed to working in modules, but much of it involves schools or teachers operating separately from each other.

- The "information and communication technologies" pump: there is a powerful potential for ICT to transform education, but its use in schools remains underdeveloped, partly because the main *modus operandi* of school administration and instruction are resistant to change.

📖 *Innovation in the Knowledge Economy: Implications for Education and Learning*, 2004, Chapter 2.

Too much of educational decision-making is preoccupied by the short term: Today's world is increasingly complex and uncertain, with a growing number of stakeholders making new demands on education. Yet, so much of education is still determined by short-term thinking – preoccupation with pressing immediate problems or simply seeking more efficient ways of maintaining established practice. Neglect of the long term is increasingly problematic in meeting the challenges of complexity and change. Futures thinking can stimulate reflection on the major changes taking place in education and its wider environment. It helps to clarify visions of what schooling should be and how to get there, and the undesirable futures to avoid. As well as clarifying values and options, it provides tools to engage in strategic dialogue.

📖 *Think Scenarios, Rethink Education*, 2006, Foreword and Part 2.

9.2. Orientations for policy

The "Schooling for Tomorrow" Rotterdam conference included policy orientations on "Fostering and Disseminating Innovation". Among the orientations for policy were:

- **Bold experimentation, evaluation, and dissemination:** A climate of experimentation should be fostered within the broad frameworks of national goals, with imaginative solutions devised for the real challenges being confronted on the ground. Evaluation and feedback are critical... We lack good dissemination strategies, and these are a priority.

- **Sustaining innovation and improvement:** There should be high levels of support for successful innovation and experimentation to ensure that the benefits are sustainable. Those facing the greatest challenges, in situations of compound disadvantages, most need that support.

📖 *Networks of Innovation: Towards New Models for Managing Schools and Systems*, 2003, Chapter 9.

Effective decision-making means to be informed as far as possible by evidence with educational professionals working in a "knowledge-rich" environment: There is need for better links between educational research, policy and practice and for further progress towards making education knowledge-rich for its professionals. Greater access to web-based information goes hand-in-hand with less quality control, alongside a shift in most OECD countries towards more decentralised decision-making in education. Given greater information, less quality control, a more informed public, and a greater diversity of policy makers, the need for clear, reliable, and easily available evidence on which to base decisions has become more important than ever before, as has the need to find mechanisms to obtain reliable answers to pressing policy questions.

📖 *Evidence in Education: Linking Research and Policy*, 2007, Chapter 1.

Create and encourage knowledge brokerage in education systems: Brokerage agencies are increasingly important to encourage dialogue between policy makers, researchers and educators and to build capacity to evaluate what does and does not work. An important first step is to create a database of quality research on key topics of interest to policy makers and to provide clear goals for conducting and evaluating educational research. A key component of these brokerage agencies is the transparent exchange of findings with their methodologies clearly defined, with commitment to update and maintain state-of-the-art syntheses on core topics. And, all agencies should seek to disseminate to as wide an audience as possible in order to effect both top-down and bottom-up change.

📖 *Evidence in Education: Linking Research and Policy*, 2007, Chapter 1.

A "template" to assess the adequacy of each system's research and development in education has been developed and refined in the course of an OECD series of R&D reviews:

- **Defining aims and challenges for educational R&D:** What is the political, economic, social and cultural context of the country? What are the country's aspirations and strategies for development? What is the nature of the country's existing educational R&D? What are the major contemporary challenges to the country's educational R&D?

- **Strategic awareness about R&D, system-wide and by key stakeholders:** What is the extent and quality of the country's current knowledge about its own educational system? What provision is there for the accumulation and organisation of existing educational knowledge (basic, applied and developmental) in the country? How committed are the country's key stakeholders to the introduction of a national system for managing the production and use of educational evidence and knowledge? Does the country have a national policy or strategy for educational R&D, with a clear definition of what counts as basic and applied research and what counts as forms of development by practitioners and others?

- **A sound base of basic research:** Does the country have appropriate provisions and incentives for the production of high quality and innovative basic research?

- **Flourishing applied research:** Does the country have appropriate provisions and incentives for the production of high quality and relevant applied research? How are researchers, policy makers, practitioners and other appropriate stakeholders in the country engaged in the identification, development, application and evaluation of national priorities for applied research and for development?

- **Development and professional enquiry:** Does the country have appropriate provisions and incentives for the production of high quality and relevant development work, professional enquiry and improvement, and how is it embedded in the education and training of practitioners?

- **Systemic issues – co-ordination, connectedness, communication, dissemination, capacity building:** How are the country's various research and development activities distributed, networked and co-ordinated nationally? How is the country's research and development work linked to appropriate international networks, centres and activities? What quality assurance and accountability procedures are in place for the country's educational research and development? What provision is there for the communication and dissemination of research findings to the country's stakeholders, including the general public, and how effective is this knowledge transformation and transfer? Is there adequate capacity building to sustain the country's complementary forms of educational research and development?

📖 "National Reviews of Educational R&D Systems – Switzerland", 2007.

ISBN 978-92-64-05989-4
Education Today
The OECD Perspective
© OECD 2009

Bibliography

OECD titles

OECD (2000), *From Initial Education to Working Life: Making Transitions Work*, OECD Publishing, Paris.

OECD (2001), *Education Policy Analysis – 2001 Edition*, OECD Publishing, Paris.

OECD (2001), *Designs for Learning: 55 Exemplary Educational Facilities*, OECD Publishing, Paris.

OECD (2003), *Education Policy Analysis – 2003 Edition*, OECD Publishing, Paris.

OECD (2003), *Student Engagement at School: A Sense of Belonging and Participation. Results from PISA 2000*, OECD Publishing, Paris.

OECD (2003), *Networks of Innovation: Towards New Models for Managing Schools and Systems*, OECD Publishing, Paris.

OECD (2003), *New Challenges for Educational Research*, OECD Publishing, Paris.

OECD (2003), *Students with Disabilities, Learning Difficulties and Disadvantages: Statistics and Indicators*, OECD Publishing, Paris.

OECD (2004), *Learning for Tomorrow's World: First Results from PISA 2003*, OECD Publishing, Paris.

OECD (2004), "Lifelong Learning", *Policy Brief*, OECD Publishing, Paris.

OECD (2004), *Education at a Glance: OECD Indicators – 2004 Edition*, OECD Publishing, Paris.

OECD (2004), *Disability in Higher Education*, OECD Publishing, Paris.

OECD (2004), *Completing the Foundation for Lifelong Learning: An OECD Survey of Upper Secondary Schools*, OECD Publishing, Paris.

OECD (2004), *Internationalisation and Trade in Higher Education: Opportunities and Challenges*, OECD Publishing, Paris.

OECD (2004), *Quality and Recognition in Higher Education: The Cross-border Challenge*, OECD Publishing, Paris.

OECD (2004), *Career Guidance and Public Policy: Bridging the Gap*, OECD Publishing, Paris.

OECD (2004), *Innovation in the Knowledge Economy: Implications for Education and Learning*, OECD Publishing, Paris.

OECD (2004), *Co-financing Lifelong Learning: Towards a Systemic Approach*, OECD Publishing, Paris.

OECD (2004), "Improving Skills for More and Better Jobs: Does Training Make a Difference?", *Employment Outlook – 2004 Edition*, OECD Publishing, Paris, Chapter 4.

OECD (2005), *Education at a Glance: OECD Indicators – 2005 Edition*, OECD Publishing, Paris.

OECD (2005), "OECD Recommendation Concerning Guidelines on Earthquake Safety in Schools", OECD Publishing, Paris.

OECD (2005), *Promoting Adult Learning* (with the Directorate for Employment, Labour and Social Affairs), OECD Publishing, Paris.

OECD (2005), *E-Learning in Tertiary Education: Where do We Stand?*, OECD Publishing, Paris.

OECD (2005), *Teachers Matter: Attracting, Developing and Retaining Effective Teachers*, OECD Publishing, Paris.

OECD (2005), *Formative Assessment: Improving Learning in Secondary Classrooms*, OECD Publishing, Paris.

OECD (2005), *Students with Disabilities, Learning Difficulties, and Disadvantages: Statistics and Indicators*, OECD Publishing, Paris.

OECD (2005), *ICT and Learning: Supporting Out-of-School Youth and Adults*, OECD Publishing, Paris.

OECD (2005), *Education Policy Analysis – 2004 Edition*, OECD Publishing, Paris.

OECD (2005), "Alternatives to Universities Revisited", *Education Policy Analysis – 2004 Edition*, OECD Publishing, Paris, Chapter 1.

OECD (2005), "Getting Returns from Investing in Educational ICT", *Education Policy Analysis – 2004 Edition*, OECD Publishing, Paris, Chapter 2.

OECD (2005), "How Well Do Schools Contribute to Lifelong Learning?", *Education Policy Analysis – 2004 Edition*, OECD Publishing, Paris, Chapter 3.

OECD (2006), *Education at a Glance: OECD Indicators – 2006 Edition*, OECD Publishing, Paris.

OECD (2006), *Starting Strong II: Early Childhood Education and Care*, OECD Publishing, Paris.

OECD (2006), *Think Scenarios, Rethink Education*, OECD Publishing, Paris.

OECD (2006), *Where Immigrant Students Succeed: A Comparative Review of Performance and Engagement in PISA 2003*, OECD Publishing, Paris.

OECD (2006), "E-learning in Tertiary Education", *Policy Brief*, OECD Publishing, Paris.

OECD (2006), *Education Policy Analysis – 2006 Edition*, OECD Publishing, Paris.

OECD (2006), *Demand-sensitive Schooling? Evidence and Issues*, OECD Publishing, Paris.

OECD (2007), *Higher Education and Regions: Globally Competitive, Locally Engaged*, OECD Publishing, Paris.

OECD (2007), *Education at a Glance: OECD Indicators – 2007 Edition*, OECD Publishing, Paris.

OECD (2007), *Understanding the Social Outcomes of Learning*, OECD Publishing, Paris.

OECD (2007), *Evidence in Education: Linking Research and Policy*, OECD Publishing, Paris.

OECD (2007), *Understanding the Brain: The Birth of a Learning Science*, OECD Publishing, Paris.

OECD (2007), "National Reviews of Educational R&D Systems – Switzerland", OECD Publishing, Paris.

OECD (2007), *Qualifications Systems: Bridges to Lifelong Learning*, OECD Publishing, Paris.

OECD (2007), *No More Failures: Ten Steps to Equity in Education* (by Simon Field, Malgorzata Kuczera and Beatriz Pont), OECD Publishing, Paris.

OECD (2007), *PISA 2006 – Volume 1: Analysis*, OECD Publishing, Paris.

OECD (2008), *Students with Disabilities, Learning Difficulties and Disadvantages: Policies, Statistics and Indicators*, OECD Publishing, Paris.

OECD (2008), *Teaching, Learning and Assessment for Adults: Improving Foundation Skills* (by Janet Looney), OECD Publishing, Paris.

OECD (2008), *Improving School Leadership – Volume 1: Policy and Practice* (by Beatriz Pont, Deborah Nusche and Hunter Moorman), OECD Publishing, Paris.

OECD (2008), *Tertiary Education for the Knowledge Society* (two volumes) (by Paulo Santiago, Karine Tremblay, Ester Basri and Elena Amal), OECD Publishing, Paris.

OECD (2008), *Education at a Glance: OECD Indicators – 2008 Edition*, OECD Publishing, Paris.

OECD (2008), *Higher Education to 2030 – Volume 1: Demography*, OECD Publishing, Paris.

Co-produced by OECD and other titles

Coulombe *et al.* (2004), *International Adult Literacy Survey, Literacy Scores, Human Capital and Growth across Fourteen OECD Countries*, Statistics Canada, Ottawa.

OECD and Canadian Policy Research Networks (CPRN) (2005), *From Education to Work: A Difficult Transition for Young Adults with Low Levels of Education*.

OECD/UNESCO (2005), *Guidelines for Quality Provision in Cross-border Higher Education*, Paris.

Ok, W. and P. Tergeist (2003), "Improving Workers' Skills: Analytical Evidence and the Role of the Social Partners", *OECD Labour Market and Social Policy Occasional Papers*, No. 10, Paris.

Statistics Canada and OECD (2005), *Learning a Living: First Results of the Adult Literacy and Life Skills Survey*, Ottawa and Paris.

World Bank (2005), *World Development Report 2006*, World Bank and Oxford University Press.

OECD PUBLISHING, 2, rue André-Pascal, 75775 PARIS CEDEX 16
PRINTED IN FRANCE
(96 2009 02 1 P) ISBN 978-92-64-05989-4 – No. 56653 2009